Living Questions

Living Questions

SUE HASTED

Editor: GEOFF TEECE

Stanley Thornes (Publishers) Ltd

Text © Sue Hasted 1993

Original illustrations by
© Stanley Thornes (Publishers) Ltd 1993

All rights reserved. No part of this publication may be reproduced or transmitted in any form or by any means, electronic or mechanical, including photocopy, recording, or any information storage and retrieval system, without permission in writing from the publisher or under licence from the Copyright Licensing Agency Limited. Further details of such licences (for reprographic reproduction) may be obtained from the Copyright Licensing Agency Limited, of 90 Tottenham Court Road, London WIP 9HE.

The rights of Sue Hasted and Geoff Teece to be identified as authors of this work have been asserted by them in accordance with the Copyright, Designs and Patents Act 1988.

First published in 1993 by:
Stanley Thornes (Publishers) Ltd
Ellenborough House
Wellington Street
CHELTENHAM GL50 1YD
England

A catalogue record for this book is available from the British Library.

ISBN 0-7487-16254

Typeset by Tech-Set, Gateshead, Tyne & Wear
Printed and bound in Hong Kong

Living Questions forms part of the *Westhill Project R.E. 5-16* materials. However, *Living Questions* is also intended to be used independently of the *Westhill Project*.

Designer Claire Brodmann
Editor Caroline Sheldrick
Artists Gillian Hunt, Sarah Jowsey and Mike Miller

Acknowledgements

The authors and publisher gratefully acknowledge permission from copyright holders to reproduce material as follows:
Amaravati Publications for extract on p. 43 from *Mindfulness: The Path to the Deathless* by Ajahn Sumedho (Amaravati Publications, 1987); Harper & Row Inc. for extract on p. 56 from *Pilgrim at Tinker Creek* by Annie Dillard (Harper & Row, 19??);
Alfred Knopf Inc. for two extracts on p. 63 from *How Can I Help?* by Ram Dass and Paul Gorman (A Knopf Inc. USA, 1985); and The Leprosy Mission of Goldhay Way, Orton Goldhay, Peterborough PE2 5GZ, for extract on p. 45 from *New Day* Magazine (Autumn 1991).

The authors and publisher gratefully acknowledge permission to reproduce copyright photographs on the following pages:

Allsport/Gray Mortimore p. 54; Amaravati Buddhist Centre p. 43 (bottom); Andes Press/Peter Grant p. 41, Andes Press/Carlos Reyes p. 11, p. 13 (bottom), p. 39, p. 46 (bottom); Barnaby's Picture Library p. 18, p. 25 (bottom), p. 31 (bottom), p. 45 (bottom), p. 46 (top); David Bocking p. 20; Bridgeman Art Library p. 9 (bottom); The British Library Oriental and India Office Collections p. 9 (top); Camera Press/Charles Ward p. 52, Camera Press/Geoff Howard p. 57 (top); Jonathan Cheshire p. 58; CIRCA Photo Library p. 19 (bottom), p. 48; Format/Sheila Gray p. 21, Format/Joanne O'Brien p. 29 (top), Format/Mo Wilson p. 61; Hutchinson Library/Felicity Nock p. 29 (bottom); Camilla Jessell p. 57 (bottom); The Leprosy Mission p. 45 (top); Mary Evans Picture Library p. 32; Ocean Youth Club p. 40 (top); Ann and Bury Peerless p. 63; Science Photo Library p. 8, p. 10 (bottom), p. 14, p. 15 (both); Scope Features p. 10 (top); Screen Ventures p. 31 (top); Geoff Teece p. 40 (bottom); Jerry Wooldridge p. 12, p. 13 (top), p. 16, p. 17, p. 19 (top), p. 25 (top), p. 38 and p. 43 (top).

CONTENTS

Introduction   7

1 THE NATURAL WORLD
What are we doing on Earth?   8
Are there miracles and mysteries?   10
Chance or destiny?   12
Is the world full of wonders?   14

2 CELEBRATIONS
What do we celebrate?   16
How do we celebrate?   18
Why do we celebrate?   20
Who do we celebrate with?   22

3 RELATIONSHIPS
Are we unique?   24
Alone or together?   26
Why do conflicts happen?   28
Breaking up or making up?   30

4 STAGES OF LIFE
What is life for?   32
What shall we do next?   34
What's the right thing to do?   36
Is the time right?   38

5 LIFESTYLES
What is 'the good life'?   40
Here and now or hereafter?   42
What improves the quality of life?   44
What threatens the good life?   46

6 RULES
Why do we have rules?   48
What do the rules really mean?   50
Are there any rules which never change?   52
What happens to rule breakers?   54

7 SUFFERING
What is suffering?   56
Has suffering a place?   58
Can suffering be a means to an end?   60
How can we cope with suffering?   62

Index   64

INTRODUCTION

You might like to start using this book by looking briefly at all the questions at the top of the pages. Have you ever found yourself asking questions like these?

The book is called *Living Questions* because it is organised around the kinds of questions all human beings ultimately ask about being alive. The title also shows that the questions themselves are very much alive. People ask them today, and will ask them in future, just as they did hundreds of years ago.

Questions such as 'Where did the universe come from?' 'Why are we here?' and 'Is there a purpose for human life?' are most often answered by beliefs of some kind, and very often by religious beliefs. Investigating the answers that different faiths have given to these basic questions is one way of discovering what matters most to each faith tradition. Knowing what is most important to each tradition makes it easier to understand why each has particular religious practices. You may already have learned about many of these as part of your religious education.

Developing our knowledge about beliefs, including our own, helps us to focus our ideas and express them more clearly. Exploring and expressing our own responses to ideas about the spiritual side of life helps us to grow in awareness and develop a thoughtful approach to life. If we learn why people believe certain things, what they think is important in life, and how they make their lives meaningful, we understand them – and ourselves – all the better.

1 THE NATURAL WORLD

What are we doing on Earth?

Think for a moment about where we are. We live on Earth, a small planet, warmed by a huge hydrogen explosion we call the Sun. Together we are swinging around the universe in one of the spiral arms of a galaxy containing many suns. Our galaxy is one of a hundred thousand million galaxies in the known universe. And we human beings are able to be aware of such things, and try to make sense of them.

Q **Can you imagine nothing at all existing? Do you find surprising the idea that the universe exists at all?**

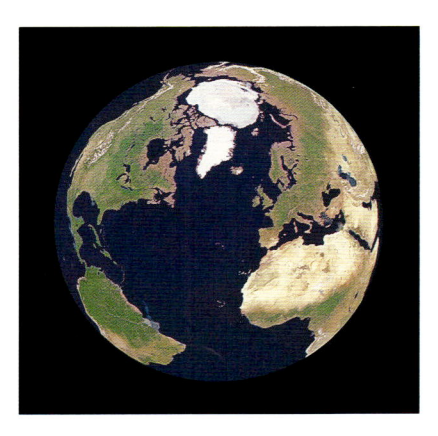

The Earth – a computer image from satellite information

The Earth's history
15 billion years condensed into a year

First hundred-millionth of a second: the Big Bang
25 minutes later: universe cools; stable atoms form
February/March: gas clouds condense into galaxy clusters
September: our Sun and solar system formed from debris of explosion
October: simple algae and bacteria appear on Earth
November: complex cells evolve
December: first creatures with backbones crawl out of sea
25 December to midday 30 December: dinosaurs rule
Midday 31 December: apes (our ancestors) evolve
One-and-a-half minutes to midnight: human language develops
30 seconds to midnight: farming begins
Five to seven seconds to midnight: Buddha and Christ alive
Half a second to midnight: the Industrial Revolution in Britain
One-tenth of a second to midnight: World War II

Condensed from Peter Russell *The Awakening Earth*

There are several ways in which we can explain why we live on Earth and how we got here. One way is to use science. Science deals in matters of fact. It is concerned with ideas which can be proved by test to be either true or false. Using science, we have built up a very useful picture of the way things work.

Q **Name as many branches of science as you can. What do they investigate?**

Science has certainly helped people make material progress. It has enabled us to produce more food, medicines and machines, for example. At a basic level, science draws a picture of the world that we find useful. In the box is a description of the history of the Earth, put together from information provided by scientists working in different fields.

Q **What does this picture tell us about the place of human beings in the universe? Does it make us seem special in any way?**

THE NATURAL WORLD

Another way of looking at our place in the universe is through the eyes of religion. Most world religions have stories about the creation of the universe and the Earth. In the Hindu creation story, we are told that this is but one of many universes created by Brahman, the supreme God. Each universe is destroyed by the god Shiva while Brahman sleeps; when he wakes it is recreated and maintained by the god Vishnu. It is an endless cycle of creation and destruction. Human lives follow the same pattern.

Jews and Christians can read two stories in the Bible about God creating the Earth and the heavens in six days (Genesis 1 and 2). The first man and woman were given authority over all living things.

Some religious people believe these stories tell the literal, historic truth. Many others see them as fables, or myths, full of meaning but not literally true. Either way, they are important, giving us a picture of the place of human beings in the scheme of things.

Q **Do you know any other creation stories? What does each tell us about the role of human beings?**

These days, many of us tend to think of the scientific way of describing the world as common sense. Even if we are members of a religious group, we may accept some scientific explanations. For example, the Catholic Church agrees that a 'Big Bang' or cosmic explosion could indeed have been the start of the universe, but would say that the Big Bang was created by God. Whatever the origin of the universe, human beings find themselves on Earth and try to make sense of their lives.

Q **Do you think there is a purpose for the universe or the world? Are human beings the purpose of the evolution of life on Earth? Or are we simply another life-form, like the dinosaurs?**

In the rest of this section, we will be looking at some of the ways in which people see and explain aspects of the natural world, and raise questions about them.

Adam and Eve, the first man and woman in the Bible creation story

THE NATURAL WORLD

Are there miracles and mysteries?

There are many mysterious events that happen in the universe. We try to explain them in different ways. Some we recognise as deliberate deceptions, like those which are used by 'magicians'. Conjurors trick us into thinking we see something that is not actually going on; they deal in illusions.

Illusions are not always created deliberately by someone trying to deceive us. They can be created by our own perceptions - the way we sense things - or how we interpret our perceptions. Have you heard of a mirage? It occurs when a shimmering heat haze bends, or refracts, light in such a way that we see a distorted image of a faraway object as if it is near. Gasping travellers on camels see a lake and palm trees just over the next sand-dune: but the real lake is far, far away.

How does magician Jeffrey Durham do it?

Q **What is it that makes people all over the world enjoy magic tricks? Is it to do with trying to guess how they really work?**

Q **Is there always a reality behind every illusion? How can you tell when something is an illusion?**

However, some people really believe in unseen forces or special powers. Sometimes these may be natural forces that are not well understood: water diviners, who use a hazel rod or a pendulum to sense underground water, may be using a simple, natural power that scientists do not yet understand. Some people say that they can see the future by looking at a person's hand or a crystal ball or cards. Some, such as 'witches', claim even greater powers.

Q **What examples of these kinds of magic do you know of? Do you think any of them are dangerous or bad? Do you think science can sometimes produce dangerous or bad results?**

There is no question about it; some things *are* mysterious. Over recent years, strange circular patterns like this one have been seen in crop fields all over the world. The corn has been flattened in a whirl with very distinct edges. The shapes usually appear overnight, and apart from a couple of obvious hoaxes, whoever or whatever makes them remains a mystery.

Crop circle in Hampshire

THE NATURAL WORLD

All kinds of suggestions have been put forward by way of explanation. Could it be deer dancing in circles? Anti-matter? Aliens landing in UFOs? Some ideas are based on scientific principles; others are based on theories which science cannot support.

Q **Do you know of any other mysterious happenings that have not been completely explained? Have you ever experienced anything of this sort?**

Sometimes mysteries are called 'miracles', especially when they have a happy result. We might say 'it's a miracle!' if someone survives a terrible accident, for example. Our logical minds tell us that they should have died; we cannot quite explain why, in spite of everything, they are still alive.

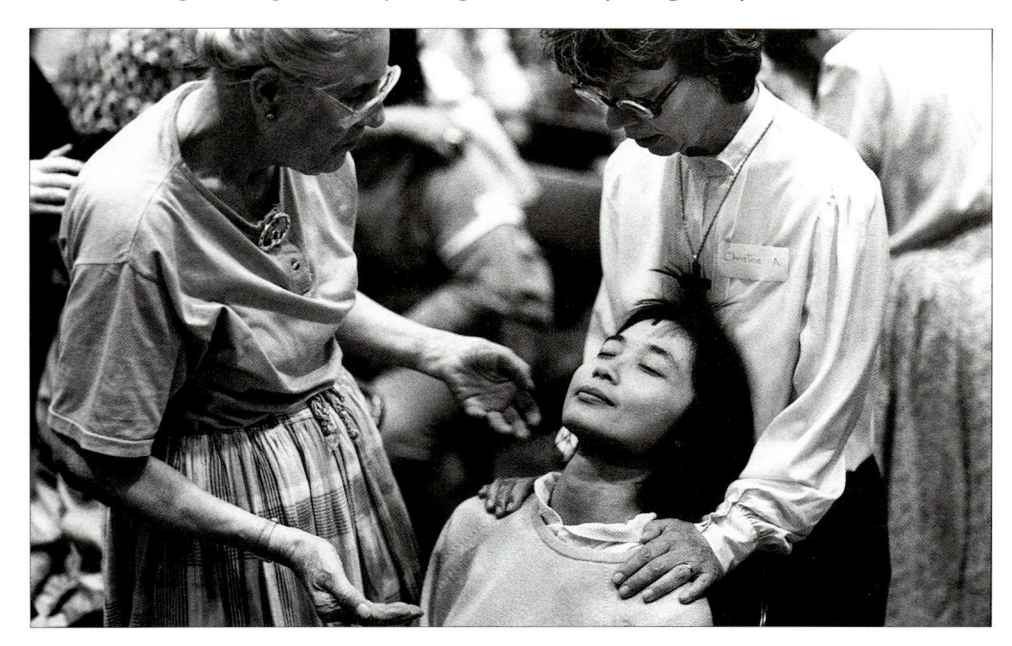

Some 'miracles' are particularly hard to explain. For instance, some people claim to be able to heal others, without the use of medicines or surgery, often by touching them. This can be part of a religious ceremony of some sort, but sometimes it is simply an encounter between the two people involved.

Christians believe Jesus was a healer. What follows is one of the stories from the Bible about his healing power.

> Even as he spoke there came a president of the synagogue, who bowed low before him and said, 'My daughter has just died; but come and lay your hand on her, and she will live.' Jesus rose and went with him, and so did his disciples. Then a woman who had suffered from haemorrhages [bleeding] for twelve years came up from behind, and touched the edge of his cloak; for she said to herself, 'If I can only touch his cloak, I shall be cured.' But Jesus turned and saw her, and said 'Take heart, my daughter; your faith has cured you.' And from that moment she recovered.
>
> When Jesus arrived at the president's house and saw the flute-players and the general commotion, he said, 'Be off! The girl is not dead: she is asleep'; and they only laughed at him. But, when everyone had been turned out, he went into the room and took the girl by the hand, and she got up. This story became the talk of all the country round.
>
> Matthew 9:18–25

Q **Can you think of any modern happenings that you would call miracles? Why would you call them miracles, rather than just happy events? Do you have any explanation for them?**

THE NATURAL WORLD

Chance or destiny?

Sometimes people have a feeling that the events that happen to them are not just chance. They may say things like 'it's my destiny' or 'I was fated to do that'. But is the universe and everything that happens in it planned beforehand, so that we have no choice but to follow our 'destiny'? We are obviously subject to physical laws in the universe: try resisting the force of gravity, for example! But does this mean that we have no freedom of action, like leaves blown about by the wind? Most people seem to believe that, to some extent, we are free to choose one path rather than another.

Hindu astrologers use a chart and read palms

Astrologers believe that there is a connection between individual lives and the universe as a whole. The astrological chart, or horoscope, is a complex astronomical map, based on the date, year, time and place of a person's birth. The sun, moon and planets are all given values relating to aspects of people's characters. Since you act according to your character, your life will naturally follow a certain line of development. Some people are against astrology because it seems to say that we are fated to act as we do and have no choice about it. Serious astrologers say that the aim of astrology is to help people to know themselves, so that they can express their unique characters in the best possible ways. But many people use horoscopes to find out what the future holds for them.

Q *Do you ever read your horoscope in magazines or newspapers? Do you believe that there could be some relationship between the positions of the planets at your birth and your character?*

Astrologers say that our fate is not 'predestined': in other words, that the events of our lives, and of the world, are not determined in advance down to the last detail. But they also say that 'free will' – our ability to decide what we do, to shape our own fate – is an illusion, because we are part of the world and cannot act separately from it.

Q *Do you think we are free to choose what we do? Or is everything determined in advance?*

The same problem arises if you believe, as many people do, that God created everything and planned everything that has ever happened and ever will happen. If this is the case, then did God also plan everything that humans will ever do? After all, we are part of the universe.

At first glance, this may not seem to be a problem. We may be happy to think about all the good things God created and planned, such as the beauty of flowers and trees, the love of families, the kindness that some people show for others, and so on. But did God also create and plan all the things we find bad? What about ugliness and pain and misery? What about all the bad things humans do to each other: are they all part of God's plan, determined in advance?

THE NATURAL WORLD

Praying five times each day helps Muslims to be aware of Allah

The conflict between free will and 'determinism' is an issue for all the major world religions. Muslims, for example, believe that God, who created us, is all-powerful and all-knowing. But God created people who can be both good and evil and allows them to choose which path to follow. After death, there will be a judgement of their behaviour.

For Muslims, faith in God, felt in the heart, transforms the mind, beliefs and actions. Muslims believe that if they remember God constantly, it is then possible to choose to live a good life. For this reason they stop to pray at set times each day, and study the Qur'an, which helps them to learn what kinds of actions are good.

Q **Do you know what any of the other religions has to say about free will?**

Where do bad deeds come from? Some believers say there is a force for evil, sometimes called the Devil, who tempts humans away from good and causes bad things to happen. But if God created everything in the universe, did he also create the Devil?

Q **Where do you think evil comes from? Are people made to do bad things by some outside force, or do they freely choose to do them?**

Most of us believe that what we decide to do can change the world. For example, this animal rights protester thinks she can persuade people to change their minds about how they treat animals. She may also have decided not to eat meat, and perhaps she does not wear leather or fur, or use products that have been tested on animals. She is acting on her beliefs.

Q **Can we decide whether to be good or bad, or is our behaviour just part of the cosmic plan? If our behaviour is all predestined, can we be held responsible for anything we do?**

Marchers protest against animal experiments

THE NATURAL WORLD

Is the world full of wonders?

You have probably heard of the Seven Wonders of the World, but do you know what any of them were? Look at the list in the box and see how many you recognise.

THE SEVEN WONDERS OF THE WORLD

- The pyramids in Egypt
- The Hanging Gardens of Semiramis at Babylon
- The Temple of Diana at Ephesus
- Phidias's statue of Jupiter at Athens
- The Mausoleum at Helicarnassus
- The Colossus at Rhodes
- The Pharos (lighthouse) at Alexandria

Q *This list was compiled in the second century BCE by Philo of Byzantium, a scientist. What do these wonders all have in common?*

There are many man-made, and woman-made, things in the world that you might consider marvellous. If you were to choose your own seven items, what would you choose? The tallest building in the world? The huge dam at Aswan in Egypt? The latest space vehicle? Perhaps you might consider a list of human achievements, instead of objects. You could choose from the fields of science, art or sport, for example. And what about humanitarian achievements: ways in which people have helped others?

Q *Make your own list of seven modern wonders. You could use a book of records to help you. Why do the ones you have chosen seem marvellous to you?*

Q *Now think about the natural wonders of the world: things that simply exist, and are not made by humans. What do you find the most amazing? Can you list ten items?*

At a microscopic level, all kinds of processes go on that we may well be unaware of.

Q *Does it seem wonderful to you, for example, that life can start from a single cell, which divides again and again to make a new creature?*

These small house dust mites are all around us. They live on human skin flakes, which we shed all the time. Your mattress is likely to contain as many as 10 000 of these creatures. A few people are allergic to them, but most of us live with them happily.

THE NATURAL WORLD

Nature makes use of a small number of patterns, which are varied in many different ways. A photograph of a river delta taken from the air can look like a painting of a tree trunk and branches. A shell can resemble a goat's horns, or a storm, or a spiral galaxy.

> **Q** **Why do you think there are patterns in nature? Is this order evidence that the world has been created by an intelligent being, or is it just a random arrangement of matter?**

When we move into the world of natural forces, there are many still unexplained. We use some of the forces, such as electromagnetism, in our daily lives, when we turn on a radio or a light. We know that if we jump in the air we will come down to Earth, because of gravity. We know how to make nuclear power stations and nuclear bombs. But although scientists have theories which can account for the way most of these forces work on their own, no one has yet discovered a grand theory which will explain how everything works at the same time.

> **Q** **Does knowing that science cannot explain everything make you feel differently about it?**

The following story comes from the Zen Buddhist tradition. Zen is a form of meditation which aims to free the mind from attachment to things and ideas about things.

> Hogen, a Chinese Zen teacher, lived alone in a small temple in the country. One day, four travelling monks appeared and asked if they might make a fire in his yard to warm themselves. While they were building the fire, Hogen heard them arguing about whether you can ever really separate your knowledge of a thing from yourself, the knower. He joined them and said 'There is a big stone over there. Do you consider it to be inside or outside your mind?'
>
> One of the monks replied: 'From the Buddhist viewpoint, it's only the mind that divides one thing from another, the stone from everything else. So I would say that the stone is inside my mind.' 'Your head must feel very heavy,' observed Hogen, 'if you are carrying around a stone like that in your mind.'
>
> Adapted from 'The Stone Mind' in *Zen Flesh, Zen Bones*, compiled by Paul Reps

Similar natural patterns: the spirals of a fossil shell and a severe storm

In Buddhism, it is said that as long as we try to explain things, we are bound by *karma*, trapped in our own framework or picture of the world. When we give up attempts to explain, we are free to understand the whole of life.

> **Q** **Do you think it will ever be possible to understand the universe? Is it more likely, do you think, that we can understand it in a religious way than in any other?**

2 CELEBRATIONS

What do we celebrate?

It's your birthday. You have made it through another year. What are you going to do on your birthday? Will you have a party, with special food, a cake and candles? Or will you go somewhere special for a treat: a theme park, perhaps? What about presents and cards? Will your friends and relations surprise you?

In this section, we shall be looking at various celebrations more closely. We shall consider what people do when they celebrate, why they celebrate, and who they celebrate with. But first, what do we mean by 'celebrate'?

We humans spend a lot of our time celebrating at different stages of our lives. When we are born, there is usually some sort of celebration of our safe arrival. We celebrate our arrival at adulthood, our partnership with another adult in marriage, and later, our deaths: at least, other people do! A celebration is a way of formally recognising an event. It can be the recognition of major life changes such as these. We also celebrate 'one-off' occasions such as a sporting win, or the end of a war, or the coronation of a new monarch.

Q *What exactly are you celebrating on your birthday? Try and think of at least three reasons to celebrate a birthday.*

Q *Why do we feel the need to mark certain occasions as special?*

Some celebrations may be held for many years, but then disappear when the need for them is no longer felt. Earlier this century, Empire Day was an annual holiday in celebration of the British Empire. Who celebrates it today? Celebrations change over time, adapting to people's needs.

Some of the occasions we celebrate regularly, such as Guy Fawkes Day, or Carnival, or Christmas, have long and complicated histories. We will look at Carnival and Christmas in more detail in the following pages.

> Guy Fawkes was a Catholic conspirator in the Gunpowder Plot of 1605, which tried, unsuccessfully, to blow up King James I in Parliament on 5 November. King James instituted a public holiday on that day in thanks for his escape from harm. But the bonfires and burning of effigies which came to be associated with Guy Fawkes Day had always happened at that time of year. They are relics of earlier Celtic festivals marking the onset of winter, some of which have also become attached to Hallowe'en.

CELEBRATIONS

Q *How many different celebrations and festivals can you think of? Brainstorm as many as you can and make a list of them.*

While you were making your list of celebrations, did you find some that you were not sure about? Some celebrations are not generally associated with happiness and laughter, bonfires or balloons. There are quite a few which have a much more solemn and sober character, in which reflection and restraint play a part, rather than feasting and merriment. One example is Remembrance Sunday in November each year, when those who died in the two world wars are remembered.

Q *What happens before and on Remembrance Sunday? Can you think of any other solemn celebrations? Add them to your list.*

Q *Now go through the list and underline any celebrations which have a religious dimension to them.*

There are many religious celebrations and festivals. Some of them recall anniversaries of the founders of faiths, such as the birthday of the Prophet Muhammad ('Eid al-Nabi) in Islam, or the enlightenment of Gautama in Buddhism. In others, the focus of attention is on historical moments, such as the initiation of the Sikh *khalsa* by Guru Gobind Singh at Baisakhi. In still others, such as Easter, Passover and Diwali, the celebrations express the central meaning of the faith for its followers, sometimes through the telling, or even acting, of a story.

Diwali celebrations

The Hindu festival of Diwali takes place in late autumn. It is a time at which the Hindu new year begins, and people settle their debts and clean their homes in readiness. Diwali is associated with the goddess Lakshmi, consort of Vishnu, who represents wealth, fortune and beauty. She is said to visit clean and brightly-lit homes and bring good fortune for the coming year. Lamps are lit in her honour, and to celebrate the story of Rama and Sita, from the Hindu poem *Ramayana*, which is retold through dance and song. Rama, the ideal king, and his beautiful wife Sita are unjustly exiled. Sita, the ideal woman, is captured by the demon king Ravana and rescued by the monkey god, Hanuman. They return in triumph to their kingdom and are welcomed by their people with lamps. Their story celebrates qualities and values which are highly esteemed in the Hindu way of life.

Q *Do you know all about the story of Rama and Sita which is acted out at Diwali? What are Rama and Sita like?*

CELEBRATIONS

How do we celebrate?

Let's look at three very different celebrations – Carnival, 'Eid ul-Fitr and Passover – and see if it is possible to find some common themes.

CARNIVAL

What is celebrated? Originally, carnival meant 'farewell to meat'. It was a Christian Roman Catholic feast held on Shrove Tuesday (or 'Mardi Gras') the day before Ash Wednesday, which is the first day of Lent. Lent is the forty-day period of fasting before Easter, the Christian celebration of the coming back to life of Jesus after his death. But as with many festivals, bits of other, older celebrations have become mixed with this one. Carnival is celebrated in many countries. In Britain it has been revived by people living in and around Notting Hill, London, whose grandparents brought the tradition to Britain from the West Indies in the 1950s. However, the date has been changed to the summer bank holiday because the British weather is usually better at that time.

How is it celebrated? In most countries, carnival is a time for music and dancing in the streets, dressing up and having fun. In Notting Hill there is a huge parade in which floats holding steel bands, competing to play the best song, lead costumed dancers along the streets. Many wear masks, and some may be dressed as devils, angels, witches and other symbolic figures. There is lots of special food and drink, and souvenirs to be bought.

Who celebrates? Although originally a Catholic festival, carnival has become a largely non-religious event involving the local community. Many visitors who go to watch find themselves joining in with the parades. In Notting Hill, the event is organised by the black community and the band floats and dancers' costumes are put together by groups within that community.

Fancy dress at Carnival

Q Look at the three festivals described. Can you identify any ways in which people mark out an occasion as special? What kinds of groups of people celebrate different occasions?

Q Make a list of the occasions you celebrate yourself. How do you celebrate them? Are there any new things you would like to celebrate? How would you go about it?

CELEBRATIONS

RAMADAN AND 'EID UL-FITR

What is celebrated? Muslim tradition holds that Ramadan was the month during which the message of God, the Qur'an, was revealed to the Prophet Muhammad, who used to pray alone in a cave on Mount Hira, near Makkah. The Qur'an requires Muslims to fast during the days of Ramadan. Fasting is one of the five 'pillars of Islam', or fundamental practices, for all Muslims.

How is it celebrated? Fasting lasts from sunrise to sunset during Ramadan, with light meals permitted after dusk and before dawn. During the day Muslims go about their usual business, but there is a special emphasis on self control: praying at the set times, curbing anger and self-indulgence. Kindness to others and charitable giving are encouraged as well as reading the Qur'an. On the first day of the next month the feast of 'Eid begins. At this time, Muslims may wear new clothes, visit family graves, exchange cards and presents and gather family and friends together to share meals.

Who celebrates? Ramadan is celebrated by the Muslim community, world-wide, in the mosque, in the family and individually.

Young Muslims wear new clothes at 'Eid ul-fitr

PASSOVER

What is celebrated? This festival, held around the end of March (Jewish *Nisan*) is focused on key events from the story of the Jews as told in the Torah: the Exodus or escape of the Jews from slavery in Egypt, the giving of the Law to the prophet Moses, and the journey through the desert to the 'promised land' of Israel. In particular, Passover celebrates the night when, in Egypt, the Angel of Death 'passed over' the houses of the Jews, but killed the first born sons of all the Egyptians, because the Pharaoh would not release the Jews from slavery.

How is it celebrated? Passover lasts for seven or eight days. The first and last days are most important, and no work is done then. Before the festival, houses are spring-cleaned and all traces of yeast are removed. Thereafter, only bread without yeast, or unleavened bread (*matzah*), is eaten. At the heart of the festival is the family *seder* meal, at which special foods are eaten, symbolising parts of the Exodus story and other important beliefs. Wine also plays a part, and hopes for the future are expressed, particularly 'next year in Jerusalem'. Sometimes songs about Jewish life and values are sung. It is a happy occasion.

Family seder meal at Passover

Who celebrates? Passover is celebrated by Jewish families, world-wide. A special role is given to children: traditionally, the youngest son asks questions at the *seder* meal and in response, the Exodus story is told.

CELEBRATIONS

Why do we celebrate?

Take a fairly simple celebration such as a birthday. You can find several reasons why people make it a special occasion: it is an opportunity for fun, for dressing up and playing games, and for eating lots of delicious food. You are telling the world that you are a whole year older and wiser. Your family are telling you that they value you and are glad you were born: they give you special presents to show you they love you. You have the chance to thank them for having you.

On Hiroshima Day, people float candle boats on rivers in memory of those who died when a nuclear bomb was dropped on the Japanese city of Hiroshima in 1945. Some celebrations draw attention to particular causes. Hiroshima Day unites people who oppose nuclear weapons.

Q **Can you think of any other celebrations which express one simple set of beliefs or values?**

Some of the major religious celebrations, which have been established and developed over long periods of time, also serve to unite people. The people drawn together by the celebration may be very different: from various backgrounds of nationality, race and culture. Even if they are religious, they may come from different branches of their faith, and may emphasise different aspects of the celebrations. Some who take part may not even be religious at all. One such celebration is the festival of Christmas.

CHRISTMAS

What is celebrated? Christians mark the birth of Jesus, whom they believe is the son of God. Jesus had a human mother, Mary, and lived a human life on Earth in order to save people from sin. The early Christians deliberately established the festival on 25 December to coincide with the Celtic winter solstice festivals. Jesus is known as 'the Light of the World', and the solstice, when the sun is at its lowest point of the year, had always been a time of celebration of fire and light. Christmas also comes at the end of the calendar year and the beginning of the new one.

CELEBRATIONS

How is it celebrated? Customs have changed over time; in these days of central heating, few people bring in a yule-log to burn from Christmas Eve through the whole twelve days of Christmas! Christian celebrations include nativity plays and special services in church, where candles may be lit and carols sung. The church may also display a crib, a model of the scene at Jesus' birth. Kindness to others and giving to charity are emphasised. Non-religious Christmas customs include decorating houses with evergreens and having a spruce tree with lights and tinsel; exchanging presents and cards with family and friends; eating a big family meal with turkey or goose, mince pies and plum pudding; playing games and sometimes watching the Queen's speech on TV. Many people take the week between Christmas and New Year's Day as holiday.

Who celebrates? Christmas is a national holiday and is recognised by national institutions (such as TV companies, with special programmes) and local ones (such as town councils, who put up street lights and trees). Christians will focus their celebrations on the church (with special services) and on the home and family. Many people who do not normally go to church may attend a family carol service or nativity play in church, or go carol-singing in aid of charity. Many non-Christians will also join in with those celebrations that are not focused on the church.

We have already seen that celebrations serve to unite people around a set of beliefs and values. People who become involved in celebrations sometimes find themselves confirming or developing beliefs and values they did not have before. Take Suzie, for example:

'My grandparents go to church, but my parents don't, except for weddings and things. Last Christmas my grandma asked me to go carol-singing with them, and I did. I liked it so much I decided to go to church with them on Sundays, and now I'm thinking about being confirmed as a Christian. I realised I wanted to have Jesus and the Holy Spirit in my life. Church has changed so much since Mum and Dad were young – I don't think they would recognise it if they came today. It's really good fun.'

Q *Choose one complex celebration (such as Christmas). Find out as much as you can about it, then answer these questions. What beliefs and values does your chosen celebration emphasise? Does everyone who joins in the celebrations hold those beliefs? Has your celebration changed over time at all? If so, why?*

CELEBRATIONS

Who do we celebrate with?

'What was I celebrating? Well, it's a secret, really. But I can tell you what I did. I went out and spent all the money I had on a big box of chocolates. I wanted to make it a special day, so I gave myself a treat.'

It is possible to celebrate on your own, but most celebrations involve other people. This is because celebrations focus on shared beliefs and values. By looking at who we celebrate with, we can sometimes work out what those shared beliefs and values are.

FAMILY

'On Mother's Day, we always get up early and make Mum breakfast in bed. We put some flowers on the tray, and her cards, and she has orange juice and a poached egg on toast and then coffee – her favourite breakfast. Then later we cook the dinner, and Mum gets to put her feet up and read the paper.'

'When it was Granny and Grandad's Golden Wedding, the whole family got together for a big party. They had four children, including Mummy, so what with the brothers' and sisters' husbands and wives and the grandchildren and a few old friends, there were 46 people altogether. Some had to travel from Southern England to get to Glasgow, and one from America – it took a bit of organising. We had a big buffet lunch and uncle Alex made a speech. We clubbed together and gave them a beautiful golden clock.'

'Friday nights we always have a special meal before the Jewish Sabbath, which is Saturday. We light candles and Father recites a prayer over the special bread and wine. He blesses Mother and us children. It's a beautiful time. We sing Hebrew songs and wish everyone a peaceful Sabbath.'

Q *What occasions do you celebrate with those you live with? Are they special to your family, or are any of them celebrated by other people too?*

FRIENDS

'We all decided to go on the Save the Whales sponsored walk together. It was good fun – we had to take a packed lunch and our wellies, and we walked nine miles. We made up songs to keep us going. And we collected over £100 between us.'

CELEBRATIONS

'On Holi, which happens at the end of February, we all go to the temple to pray and we sing songs called *bhajans*. We also chase each other and squirt coloured powder all over each other. I saved the gold for my boyfriend! We get new clothes to wear and sweets to eat, too.'

'My friends and I started a Madonna Society and on her birthday, we had a Madonna Party. Some people dressed to look like her, and we played a lot of her songs and danced for hours.'

Q What events do you celebrate with your friends? Are they different from things you would celebrate with your family? If so, why?

COMMUNITIES

'Every year our school has a fete. The aim is to raise money for books and equipment, but it's fun, too. There's usually a raffle and a tombola, and people bake cakes or bring plants and bric-a-brac to sell. This year there were pony rides on the sports field and we had a team quiz. The head teacher gave a speech and thanked all the parents for contributing to the life of the school.'

'This year the Scouts and Guides were celebrating 75 years of the local movement. We had a huge parade all round the town, followed by a short service in the local cinema – it was the only place big enough! The service was not really Christian, because there are lots of people of other faiths in the Scouts and Guides too. Our troop won a prize for the smartest uniforms and the Commissioner gave us all a lollipop.'

'When I lived in Africa as a child, we always had an Independence Day every year. It was a national holiday and there were parties and picnics and parades and fireworks in the evening. It was very exciting to be part of a new nation, trying to work together for a better future. I wish we had a day like that in Britain.'

'It always makes me feel calm and peaceful when we celebrate the Mass in church. The priest blesses the bread and wine and then we all go forward to the altar, where he gives each one the body and blood of Christ, a sip of wine and a small wafer, as Jesus commanded us in the Last Supper. There's something about the solemnity of it that makes me feel that my sins really are forgiven, and that I'm part of this greater family of the Church. It gives me the strength to keep trying to live a good life.'

Q What communities do you belong to? Do any of the communities you belong to celebrate particular things or occasions? How do they do so? What beliefs and values does each celebration focus on?

Q Are there any people you don't normally celebrate anything with, but would like to? What would you celebrate and how?

Q What beliefs and values mean most to you? Can you think of any new ways to celebrate them?

3 RELATIONSHIPS

Are we unique?

Imagine you meet a boy or girl who has just moved in next door. You want to find out about them, to see if you could become friends. You will probably ask, first of all, 'What's your name?', then 'Where did you move from?', 'How many in your family?', 'Which school are you going to?' and so on. By the time you have got down to 'What are your favourite TV programmes?' you have probably formed a pretty good idea of who they are. You will probably also have some idea of whether you could become friends or not.

Q *What makes us who we are? Are we born with our personalities already stamped into us? Or are they shaped by our relationships with other people?*

No two people are exactly the same. Most people we know have eyes, a nose and mouth, hair and so on. But we all have different shapes and colours and textures for these features. So although we can see resemblances between people, we know they are also different from each other: they are unique individuals.

Q *Choose a picture of someone in this book and try describing them. Is there anything distinctive about their appearance?*

There are other factors which make us unique. For instance, we usually speak one main language (though some people are lucky enough to grow up knowing more than one). We may think of ourselves as belonging to a particular ethnic group, perhaps because of the colour of our skin. (Actually, the line between one ethnic group and another is very difficult to draw. The latest genetic evidence shows that all humans came from the same ancestors in Africa.)

We usually belong to a nation, and that nation may, in turn, be part of a larger grouping. For instance, you may be Welsh and live in Britain, which is part of the European Community and a member of the United Nations.

Q *Does anyone in your class speak a language other than English? Are there any advantages to knowing more than one language? How many ethnic groups are represented in your class?*

RELATIONSHIPS

All of us belong to a range of groups and communities in society. Among them are the religious communities. Some people show that they belong to a particular religious tradition by wearing special clothes, like the Hasidic Jews in the picture. But all religious groups have special ways of behaving which affect their members. These are always based on their beliefs.

Q *Can you think of any ways in which believers from the major religious traditions mark themselves as belonging to their special group, by their behaviour or their appearance?*

Clothes are one way of expressing our relationship to particular communities

Apart from our membership of particular social, cultural, national and religious groups, there is another range of things that forms us as individuals. Each of us has interests we pursue: you might like reading science fiction books, or canoeing. These interests can lead to activities – you might visit a science museum or take part in a canoe rally, for example. They are usually related to our aims in life, too.

Most people have aims. They may be limited ones, such as being able to swim 200 metres, or long-term ones, such as becoming an engineer or an MP. They could be about concrete things, such as owning a guitar or a pony. Or they may be more abstract, like 'I want to be a wise person'. They could also include specifically religious aims, such as 'I want to love my neighbour as myself' or 'I want to submit my life to God's will'.

Q *What interests do you have? Do you have any aims for your future life?*

Most people do change over time; their character develops and new aims emerge. For example, you might learn another language. You could think deeply about your beliefs, and that might affect your behaviour and your aims. You might decide to leave your country and live somewhere else. Your relationships also change. Your family will certainly grow and change its membership as you grow up.

Relationships are fundamental to human life. They are a source of comfort, but they may also be a cause of conflict. In this section, we will be looking at some of the many relationships that determine who we are, and at the different attitudes of various religions to some of them. We will also examine some of the ways in which relationships can break down, and how they can be mended.

Q *Each religion has ways of expressing the aims of those who believe. Do you know of any examples that express the aims of a true Muslim, Christian, Hindu, Buddhist, Jew or Sikh?*

European flags: nations, too have to relate to one another

25

RELATIONSHIPS

Alone or together?

Meet some of the members of the Newchester Community College orchestra. They meet on Tuesdays after school to practise, but they have a number of other relationships, too. So do their families.

Q *Read the information on each person. Then make a list of all the community groups, institutions and so on you can find. Then see how many of the orchestra members belong to each group.*

JESSICA JONES

Family	Mum, an administrator at the local hospital; member of pressure group for peace
	Dad, a teacher at the Junior school; member of football club; voluntary worker for Samaritans
Interests	Swimming: goes to lessons; gardening: tends school wildflower garden; painting and drawing
Religion	None; parents are humanists
Aims	To be an artist; to travel

DAVID WHITFIELD

Family	Mum, a widow, works as a nursing sister at the hospital
	Brother in police
	Sister works at town hall; helps out at OAP's home
Interests	Scouts, camping, football, cookery: David would like to learn to cook Indian food
Religion	Christian (Baptist). David goes to Sunday school and attends Christian summer camps
Aims	To join the police; to play trumpet like Miles Davis

DEBBY GOULD

Family	Mum works part-time at bank; member of pressure group for peace
	Dad manages supermarket; member of local businesspeople's association
	Brother taking GSCEs at same school
Interests	Photography, swimming: goes to lessons; gymnastics, helping elderly people
Religion	Jewish. The family attends synagogue regularly and has twice visited Israel for holidays
Aims	To become a journalist; to live to be 'old and wise'

RELATIONSHIPS

KARIM SALEH

Family	Mum and Dad run the local post office
	Dad is a member of the local businesspeople's association and a volunteer with the Samaritans
	One sister runs playgroup for under-fives
	Another sister taking GSCEs at same school
	Older brother at university studying journalism
Interests	Cycle racing, Scouts, reading, languages: Karim speaks three already and is now learning French and German
Religion	Muslim. The family go to the local mosque
Aims	To learn ten languages; to make the pilgrimage to Makkah

RAWINDER KAUR

Family	Mum at home with younger brothers and sister; she enjoys cooking both Indian and English-style food, and helps to raise money for the hospital building fund
	Dad is a policeman; member of football club, helps at Scouts
	Two small brothers go to playgroup for under-fives
Interests	Growing things: helps with school wildflower garden; dancing, reading and films
Religion	Sikh. The family are members of the *gurdwara*, and Rawinder helps cook for the *langar*
Aims	To work in a bank; to lead the congregation in prayer; to see peace in the world

In an orchestra, the common aim of playing music serves to unify all the different musicians. Although each instrument is different, they play together in harmony. On their own, the notes of the tuba or the beats of the drum may not sound like much, but when everyone plays together, the result can be astonishing. The whole is more than the sum of its parts. Sometimes, deliberate discords can be part of the harmony.

> **Q** *What is it that makes the orchestra work? Do you think that many communities follow the pattern of an orchestra? Can you think of any examples in our society?*

Our world is made up of many overlapping communities and groups both large and small. When they share values and aims, they get along very well, and sometimes they can achieve together more than they could on their own. Perhaps we would all like to live in an ideal society, where this 'community of communities' works perfectly. The groups would then all tolerate, appreciate and accept each other's aims and activities.

> **Q** *Can there ever be such a society? What kinds of things prevent groups, communities and nations working in harmony? Are any of them related to beliefs?*

RELATIONSHIPS

Why do conflicts happen?

Do differences matter? We have seen that differences between individuals and groups can produce richer relationships, like the harmonies an orchestra produces from different instruments. But differences can also produce disharmony: clashes of temperament, beliefs and ideals.

> **Q** *What do you argue about most with your friends? Are any of your conflicts the result of different beliefs?*

Let's look at some examples of conflict in which beliefs play a central role; a personal one, a community one and a global one.

A personal conflict

Emma has asked Husain to go to the cinema with her this Friday night. She met him at school: although they are not in the same class they have known each other for three years. They enjoy each other's company and like many of the same things: the same music, books and films, for instance. They would like to go out together, but there's a big problem.

Emma is not religious. Her family long ago stopped going to church, and although she believes in God and in 'trying to be a good person', Emma does not practise any particular faith. She thinks of herself as an independent, modern girl who will have a career when she grows up and can make her own choices about who she goes out with. Her parents expect her to be sensible about her decisions, but they respect her right to make them as a free and responsible young person.

Husain, in contrast, has been brought up as a Muslim. Islam forbids men and women who are not related to each other to meet in private, for good reasons: Muslims believe that family life is very important, and must be carefully protected. Sex outside marriage is thought of as a sin. Husain's parents would like him eventually to marry a Muslim girl, preferably one they know and approve of. They don't like the idea of his going out alone with girls, particularly non-Muslim ones.

> **Q** *What are the beliefs that clash with each other here? Can you think of any solutions to Emma and Husain's problem?*

A community conflict

Political conflicts can often contain religious ingredients. Different beliefs can fan the flames of arguments which are also about territory and power. For instance, there has long been a conflict over the status of Northern Ireland, which has been divided from the Irish Republic (or Eire) since that country won its independence from Britain in the 1920s. There has been a history of struggle over the right to rule the whole country involving the religion of the rulers and the ruled, dating right back to King Henry VIII, the first Protestant (non-Catholic) British king.

Today, 95% of the population in the Republic is Roman Catholic, while in Northern Ireland, only 28% are Catholic and there are a large number of Protestants. Eire would still like to see a united Ireland, including the northern counties; but many of the Protestant majority in the north fear a takeover by a country with strongly Catholic laws and constitution, and so they remain fiercely loyal to Britain. Extremist groups on both sides of the conflict resort to violence and murder in attempts to bring about the outcome they wish for.

Catholics believe strongly in marriage, so the law in Eire makes divorce very difficult. Northern Ireland mostly follows British laws, which allow people more freedom on matters of belief.

British troops and young people in Northern Ireland

Q Do you know of any other political conflicts in which religion has a part? What are the main beliefs on each side of those conflicts?

A global conflict

The Kogi people live in Colombia, and are descendents of the people who lived in South America before it was invaded by the Spanish in the fifteenth century. They believe that the Earth is dying because humans are in conflict with it, greedily exploiting its resources. They see themselves as 'Elder Brothers' of the 'Younger Brothers' who are destroying the world, with a duty to warn us of our thoughtlessness.

Beliefs about the nature of human life and our place in the universe play a part in the world-wide conflicts over resources such as the rainforests. Are we in conflict with nature?

Q What beliefs about the role of human beings in nature do you know about?

It is useful to find out which beliefs lie at the root of conflicts. When you know what values are important to each side in a fight, it is easier to understand the problem. Once you understand the problem, you are on the road to a solution.

Q What conflicts in the world - at a local, national or global level - would you most like to see resolved? What are the problems behind them, and how might they be solved?

A man of the Kogi people of Colombia

RELATIONSHIPS

Breaking up or making up?

Conflicts happen when relationships break down. It is often sad when families and friendships break up. All the hopes for the relationship are unfulfilled, and a lot of pain and misery is involved in the process. Children often suffer as much as their parents from a broken marriage, if not more.

> **Q** **There's an old saying: 'Never let the sun set on a quarrel'. Do you agree with this? How do you go about resolving arguments with your family, or with friends?**

Christians have a clear instruction from Jesus to help them overcome conflict of any kind. It is:

'Love your enemies; do good to those who hate you; bless those who curse you; pray for those who treat you spitefully. When a man hits you on the cheek, offer him the other cheek too; when a man takes your coat, let him have your shirt as well. Give to everyone who asks you; when a man takes what is yours, do not demand it back. Treat others as you would like them to treat you.'

Luke 6:28-31

> **Q** **What would the world be like if everyone followed this advice? Can you think of any conflicts in which forgiveness would provide a solution?**

The charity Christian Aid aims to help people in the 'Third World' help themselves, through improved health, farming and manufacturing, as well as aid to refugees and the starving. It also campaigns against human rights abuses, unfair trading practices and the international arms trade: all sources of conflict.

Racism is one of the worst forms of community conflict. It can arise when one community feels threatened by another. It divides families, neighbourhoods and nations. Violent racial attacks may be based on fear and hatred of 'the others' who are seen as a threat: to jobs, homes or ways of life. Understandably, those who are the victims of such attacks may band together to defend themselves, and even hit back, creating more violence.

> **Q** **Why should people feel threatened by those of a different colour or culture? What beliefs lie behind such fears?**

RELATIONSHIPS

Islam has an answer for racism. For Muslims, the diversity of human life is given by God for a reason. We are here to learn about each other, to appreciate and respect the differences between us. If we do this, Muslims believe, our lives will be the richer.

For Muslims, the unity of human beings is a religious fact and is best expressed by a unity of religious practice. So every Muslim, regardless of race or culture, joins in daily prayers, fasting in Ramadan, and giving charity or *zakat*. Perhaps the best symbol of this unity is the wearing of *ihram*, the simple white clothes worn during the pilgrimage or *hajj* to Makkah, which show that everyone is equal before Allah.

Prophet Muhammad said 'Every Muslim is a Muslim's brother'.

Q *Do you think differences between people matter? Do you think that anything is more important than such differences?*

For Hindus, it can be more important to fight for truth than to avoid conflict. In the *Mahabharata*, a famous book of stories about the past which embody Hindu values, the heroes are warrior kings who fight to defend the truth. However, there is also a strong tradition of non-violence, or *ahimsa*, as a way through conflict.

Muslim pilgrims at Makkah

The Indian leader M K Gandhi, who lived from 1869 to 1948, practised *ahimsa* in his political struggles. He wanted to achieve freedom for India from British rule. To do this he organised non-violent boycotts, strikes and hunger strikes.

Gandhi believed that all acts of violence are based on selfishness. He thought that acting violently towards others to punish them for wrongs is like playing God, for only God knows what is right and wrong and can judge who should be punished.

The Hindu ideal of non-violence in response to conflict, which is also practised by Buddhists and Jains, is very close to the advice given by Jesus to his followers: 'Love your enemies'.

Q *Is anything worth fighting for? Which do you think is more important: non-violence, or fighting for what you believe in?*

Q *Do you know of any organisations that exist to solve conflicts, either within society or internationally? What beliefs are they based on?*

M K Gandhi

4 STAGES OF LIFE

What is life for?

We are born, we grow up, we grow old, we die. This is life for all of us, unless our lives are shortened by disaster or disease. Because we can think and feel, we usually try to make some sense of it. In the first three sections we have already looked at some of the larger questions we grapple with. But what about our individual lives? While we are here, what should we do? How should we behave? And should we behave differently at various stages in our lives?

Our first notions of the stages of life are formed by our very first relationships with those about us, by our immediate family, and then by the social groups we belong to, such as school, mosque or *gurdwara*, church or synagogue and so forth.

A spiral journey shown in an illustration from John Bunyan's Pilgrim's Progress, 1678

Many people have an image of their progress through life. One common image is that of a journey. When we are born, we set out like travellers. We take with us bits of baggage and acquire more as we travel. We visit various places where experiences befall us. Finally, we reach the end of our journey: a magical new country; or perhaps we return home again.

> **Q** *If you were to draw a line representing the pattern of a human life, what would it look like? A straight line? A curve? A circle?*

STAGES OF LIFE

Another image is that of a river, which flows from the mountains where it starts as a tiny stream, and gains size and speed as tributaries join it before it flows into the great ocean.

Life has also been likened to an hourglass, an old kind of clock which looks something like a sand-filled egg timer. The hourglass starts full of sand which trickles slowly down from the top globe to the bottom until there is none left. Life has also been compared to flowers and fields of grass, which grow up and flourish, then slowly wither and die back, only to begin anew with fresh growth the next spring. 'Life is but a dream' says the song. Great poets have called life a stage play, or a game. One Hindu symbol for life is that of a circle – a line with no ending – or a snake swallowing its own tail.

Q *Can you think of any other pictures or images that seem like life to you? Which one do you think fits best?*

Your image of what life is like will influence your ideas about what you should do with your life. If you believe, for example, that life is an accidental and meaningless time of consciousness followed by nothingness, you may decide simply to enjoy yourself as much as possible while it lasts. An anonymous writer summed it up: 'Life aint all you want. It's all you 'ave. So 'ave it!'

However, you may believe that this life is simply one among many, and that your chances of progress towards a better life next time round – or your chances of an eventual release from endless further lives – depend on your actions now. Or say you believe that when you die, your life will be judged and you will be sent to heaven or to hell. If you think about life in either of those ways, then you are likely also to feel that there are right and wrong choices to be made as you go along.

Q *Choose one of the images of life from above, and imagine how you would go about your life if you saw it in that way. What would be important to you? What sorts of things would you do with your life?*

As we have seen, human beings tend to see themselves as placed somewhere between destiny and free will. On the whole, we think that while some of the circumstances of our lives are unchangeable, we are able to choose a path through them. In this section, we will be looking at different ways in which people choose their paths.

STAGES OF LIFE

What shall we do next?

In all the stages of our lives, from birth to death, we are faced with events and circumstances to which we react. Depending on how we see life, we will react to them differently. Our outlook on life is formed, at least to begin with, by the views of our family and our immediate community. Let's look at some religious images of life and what they mean for those who hold them.

'I have a gift for maths and physics. I believe that I'm good at them because God has a purpose in mind for me. As a Christian, I believe God has created us and we are his caretakers for the world. When I'm older I shall be able to use the talent he has given me to help people. I'm very interested in space exploration, and I'd like to design rockets or satellites for peaceful purposes. I pray every day that the Holy Spirit will guide me in all things, so that I will make the right choices in my life. It's very inspiring and challenging to know that I am a part of God's plan for the progress of the world.'

'I shall be married next week to Rashid, *insha'Allah*. We say '*insha'Allah*' (if God wills) because we believe everything that happens is the will of God. I believe that God created us to worship him. We are accountable to God for everything we do; if we follow his path, revealed to Prophet Muhammad in the holy Qur'an, we will go to heaven at the end of the world. Rashid and I hope to have children – *insha'Allah* – and it will be our duty to raise them as Muslims, too. Our first words to them will be 'There is no God but Allah.' We would like to make the pilgrimage to Makkah one day.'

STAGES OF LIFE

'I am a social worker, working with kids in an inner-city area. I'm married and have kids of my own. Because I'm Jewish I believe that I must try to live my life in the spirit of God's commandments – that's our side of the agreement we have with God. He has promised to protect us and stay close to us; we have to be responsible for ourselves and everybody else in the world we find ourselves in. The kids I work with need not only love, but justice, and I hope I can work towards that for them. I think there will be some sort of judgement after our deaths – that makes what we do in this life very important.'

'My family is grown now, and I will soon be a grandmother. I now have more time to devote to the family business, and to think about my life. The Gurus told us that good Sikhs should be involved in the community, lead a useful life, and work hard and honestly. These days I have more time to think about the poor and needy, and to pass on God's blessings to other people. I believe we can draw near to God in this life, and become free and enlightened by constantly calling God to mind.'

'My family is all grown too. I have had a long life, and all through it there were responsibilities to fulfill – first to my parents, then to work, then to my wife and children. Now that I am old I feel that my first responsibility is to acquire merit, to gain good *karma* and to offset any bad things I may have done in this life. I will be making a pilgrimage to Varanasi soon. As a Hindu I meditate every day to grow closer to Brahman. I expect I shall be reborn sometime after my death – we can all expect to live many lives.'

Q If you look back at all these statements, you will find that you can divide them into two types of outlook on life. It may help you to see which type each speaker belongs to if you compare their view of life with the images of an arrow and a circle. Which image fits each speaker's beliefs more closely? Which religions do the speakers belong to?

35

STAGES OF LIFE

What's the right thing to do?

Most of us believe we can choose to do one thing rather than another: that we can decide which path to follow in life. More than that, most of us believe that by choosing a particular path of action, we can change the future of the world. Political parties are based on this idea.

Most people believe that some choices of action are better than others. However, they could have different reasons for making the same choice. For instance, someone might choose to confess to having stolen something because he knows that the police have the evidence that he did it, and he reckons he'll get a shorter sentence if he pleads guilty. Another man might confess because he feels guilty about having stolen: he believes stealing is wrong, whether you are caught or not.

Q **How do you decide what to do when you have a choice? Can you think of any big decisions you have made in your life so far? How did you make up your mind to do one thing rather than another?**

Choices arise all the time. They range from very small matters, which seem only to affect the person who is choosing, to grave matters which might affect the whole world.

Many people believe that in most situations there is a range of choices of which some are better than others. But some people say that in each case there is actually only one 'right' choice. Depending on their background, such people may believe that this choice is unavoidable, because it is fate, or the result of *karma* or past actions. Or they may believe that it is a matter of discovering the will of God, and then freely acting as God would have them do.

Shall I have a burger, or save my money and get a new pair of trainers?

In fact, all choices have consequences, even the seemingly small ones. If you eat healthy food for most meals, for example, you are less likely to suffer from heart disease when you are older. If everyone ate vegetarian food, all slaughterhouse workers would be out of a job!

Q **Can you think of any similar choices we make about our lifestyles? What consequences do they have?**

STAGES OF LIFE

Some choices are obviously very important. They demonstrate what we value most. For example, do we choose to spend more on weapons or schools? Is it more important to spend money on preventing disease, or on curing it? Should we spend more money on developing ways to travel to the stars than we do on relieving world poverty and starvation?

Q **What great choices face humankind at the moment?**

Now, we've got to pay for the armed forces, education and health. How much do we spend on each?

TIKKUN OLAM – REPAIRING THE WORLD

The following idea is found in the Jewish mystical tradition. Before the moment of creation, it is said, God's holiness filled the entire universe. At the point of creation, this holiness had to contract to allow room for the world to be. Sparks of holiness were scattered throughout the world, in all living things. It is humanity's task to observe the commandments of Torah and live in a holy way. When a person performs a good deed, a spark is reclaimed, but when a bad deed is performed, God's love is prevented from flowing into the universe. When all the holy sparks have been reclaimed from the realm of evil, the world will be redeemed.

History as choice: did we choose to develop more and more sophisticated ways of fighting? Was there any other choice?

Choices do have consequences. In a way, you can see history as a record of the choices that people made at particular times. One choice leads to a situation in which another choice is made, and so on. This means that very small choices can, in fact, lead to enormous events.

Q **Can you think of any chains of decisions and events like this in your life?**

STAGES OF LIFE

Is the time right?

The stage of life we have reached can affect our choice of action. This can simply be because youngsters have different concerns from those of older people, and more energy! For instance, you are more likely to choose to go on a long-distance hike at 13 than at 83.

> **Q** Can you think of any examples of decisions you would not make as a child, that you might make as an adult? What about the other way round?

Here, though, we are thinking about 'right' and 'wrong' actions, and the choices we make. As we have seen, what people believe is a 'good' or 'bad' action relates to their view of the purpose of life and their place in the scheme of things.

> **Q** Do you know what the words 'morality' and 'ethics' mean? What general choices of action would you label as 'immoral' or 'unethical'?

Many people feel that there are certain actions that are appropriate for particular times of life. Let's look at what this means for some people from different backgrounds.

PARVATI IS A HINDU

'We believe that there are several different ways to achieve liberation from the endless cycle of births and deaths. Myself, I follow the path of *karma yoga*. I think that our actions, or *dharma*, follow from our place in life. So this means I keep some general rules: I won't use violence or eat meat, for example, and I don't drink. But I also do particular things according to my position as a young girl, and as a Hindu in Britain today.

For instance I am respectful to my parents, and do what they say, go to temple and so on. I join in celebrations such as *rakhi*: that's when brothers and sisters tie a special bracelet on each other's wrists. And there are others which mark the stages of our growing up. I also work hard at school so that I can get a good job when I'm older. And I don't forget to have fun, too – after all, you're only young once!

Tying rakhi *bracelets*

Karma means past actions, including those in former lives. Hindus believe that *karma* influences our present life, and that our actions in this one will, in turn, influence future ones. The *Guruda Purana* says that 'Whatever is to befall a person in any particular age or time will surely overtake them then and on that date'. But although our present fate is already set, they believe, we can affect our future by choosing to act wisely. Also, Hindu astrologers sometimes predict days or times at which particular actions may be fortunate – the best day for a journey, for example.

STAGES OF LIFE

JOHN IS A CHRISTIAN

'When I was about 18 I began to feel strongly called to commit myself to the Christian life more fully. I'd been brought up a Catholic, and I went to Mass and confession all through my childhood, but I'd never really thought about being a priest until just before I left school. I suppose I was considering what to do with my life anyway, and nothing I'd looked into really felt right. One day I was sitting quietly when it just struck me very clearly that I should join the priesthood. After a while it became a very positive thing, almost a feeling that I had a vocation.'

A 'vocation', from the Latin for 'calling', means a special urge, inclination or pre-disposition to a particular career. Many Christians feel that God has a particular job for them to do in life, though not all are called to the priesthood. Such people will usually pray for help in deciding the course of their lives. Some will say they receive answers to prayer in an almost magical way: by sudden chance meetings, or even seeing visions or hearing voices. Others grow slowly into a belief about what they must do, though there may be a moment of clear understanding, as in John's experience.

Young men train to be priests at a seminary

ALI IS A MUSLIM

'As a Muslim, I certainly believe that there is an appropriate time for all actions. This is reflected in our everyday lives – we are required to pray at certain times of the day, we fast during the month of Ramadan, and so on. The aim is to be aware of Allah at all times, and to follow the example of Prophet Muhammad (peace be upon him) too. I am glad I was able to go on the *Hajj* to Makkah – it is not possible for all Muslims, although we are asked to do it.

Now that I am old, I think about my death. When it is time for me to die, I hope that someone will be there to whisper the *shahadah* in my ear, so that when my spirit is asked what it believes, I am reminded to say "There is no God but Allah, and Muhammad is God's Messenger".'

Muslims (as well as Christians and some Jews) believe that in the afterlife, our actions will be judged and we will be rewarded or punished as we deserve. This makes it important to decide on a right course of action in life, and to live life morally, because there will be no second chance to get things right.

Q Most religions have special ceremonies to mark different stages of life, particularly birth, initiation (becoming grown up), marriage and death. Do you know about any of these?

5 LIFESTYLES

What is 'the good life?'

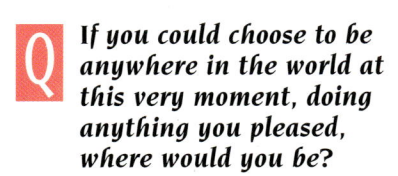

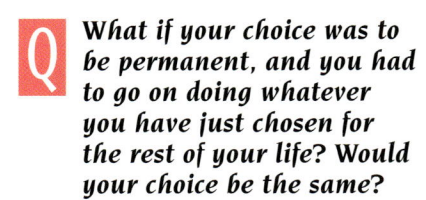

Q If you could choose to be anywhere in the world at this very moment, doing anything you pleased, where would you be?

Q What if your choice was to be permanent, and you had to go on doing whatever you have just chosen for the rest of your life? Would your choice be the same?

A sailing holiday with the Ocean Youth Club

In the last section we looked at choices and chances, and the way they affect the different stages of our lives. In this one we will be looking a little more closely at lifestyles, and at some of the beliefs reflected in the ways we choose to live.

Most of us have, in a very general way, some idea of how we would ideally like to live. We may, for instance, have a fairly clear idea of the kind of house we would like to live in, the sort of clothes we would like to wear, some of the possessions we wish we had, and some of the activities we would most like to take part in.

Wouldn't most of us like to be a just a little bit richer than we are? Then we could buy that new jacket and that bike, go on a special holiday, and maybe have enough left over to give a bit to our best friends, too...

Q What elements go to make up 'the good life' for you? How much pocket money would you ideally like to have every week? What possessions would you like to have?

The ideas we have about what things are desirable in life come from a number of different sources. An obvious one is television. We are exposed to a variety of programmes which show us images of happiness and success. Every programme selects images of success, whether it's a magazine programme with star interviews, or a soap opera with some characters who make good choices and others who don't. Often we identify with people we see on television – and in films – because we feel we would like to copy them in some way. Maybe we like the way they dress, or their looks, or the way they behave, or what they talk or sing about.

Q Who do you like? What things about them do you like most? Can you think of any ways in which you are like them?

LIFESTYLES

Television, radio and magazines also expose us to advertising for products. Often, we are encouraged to buy things which offer the possibility of a particular kind of lifestyle. Manufacturers of soft drinks, jeans and games often aim to make you think that owning their product will gain you entry into a more glamorous world where 'it's the real thing', and 'things go better' with whatever it is they want you to buy.

Q **Can you think of any advertisements which show a lifestyle that you think is attractive? Have you bought any of the things you have seen advertised?**

So our images of 'the good life' come from a variety of sources. We know what we want, and what we don't want. We don't want to be poor, usually, because we value things like a nice house, clothes and other possessions. One way we can judge the quality of our lives is by what we have. For some people – but not many – that may be the only way to judge life's quality.

Q **Are there any other ways in which we could judge the quality of life? How do we decide what other things might make up 'the good life'?**

There are many people who cannot live 'the good life' of the advertisements. They are the poor and those on very low incomes; they are the homeless; the physically or mentally disabled; those disadvantaged by the prejudices of others about their skin colour, their sex or their age. What about them? Would their idea of 'the good life' be any different?

Q **Can some of us live the good life while others are suffering? Does it matter if some are rich and others are poor?**

Q **If you are poor, does that mean you are necessarily unhappy? Can you be 'poor but happy'?**

If you have no home, it's hard to get a job.
If you have no job, you can't afford a home.

LIFESTYLES

Here and now or hereafter?

'A young man came to ask Jesus what good he must do to gain eternal life. Jesus told him to keep the commandments, but the man replied that he already did so. He asked what more he should do. Jesus told him to go and sell his possessions and give to the poor, and to follow him. The young man went away sadly, because he was rich.

'Jesus said to his disciples, "I tell you this: a rich man will find it hard to enter the kingdom of heaven. I repeat, it is easier for a camel to pass through the eye of a needle than for a rich man to enter the kingdom of God." '

Matthew 19: 23-4

Jesus also said that you cannot serve both God and money: 'Therefore I bid you put away anxious thoughts about food and drink to keep you alive, and clothes to cover your body. Surely life is more than food, and the body more than clothes. Look at the birds of the air; they do not sow and reap and store in barns, yet your heavenly Father feeds them. You are worth more than the birds!'

Matthew 6: 25-6

Because of passages from the Bible like these, Christians believe that there are more important things in life than personal possessions and material wealth. Jesus had more to say on this subject.

'Do not store up for yourselves treasure on earth, where it grows rusty and moth-eaten, and thieves break in and steal it. Store up treasure in heaven, where there is no moth and no rust to spoil it, no thieves to break in and steal. For where your treasure is, there will your heart be also.'

Matthew 6: 19-21

For Christians, it is important to think not only about our present life, but also about the future life after death. Then, they believe, there will be a judgement of our actions in this life. People will not be judged on the material success of their lives, but on the quality of their moral lives: how closely they have tried to follow Jesus's commandments.

Q **What do you know about Jesus's own lifestyle? What sort of lifestyle does a Christian try to lead? Can you think of any examples of things that a Christian might try to do with their money or possessions to use them in a Christian way?**

LIFESTYLES

Buddhists, too, have a different attitude to lifestyles from many people. The Buddhist community is divided into two groups. There are the householders – people, many with families, who have jobs and live ordinary lives – and there are monks and nuns (sometimes called *bhikkus*), who live in monasteries and spend their time meditating and teaching *dharma*, 'the truth about the way things are'.

Householders support the *bhikkus* by giving them food and helping at the monasteries. The monks and nuns live a very simple life, owning only a bowl for food, their robes, and a razor for shaving if they are men. They eat only one meal a day, own no money, and refrain from any indulgences such as ornaments, soft beds, alcoholic drinks and dancing, acting or music. This simple lifestyle was designed by the Buddha for those who wish to gain happiness: the kind of happiness that results from inner peace and calm.

Buddhist monks sit in meditation

Q **What is your definition of happiness? Is it different from the Buddhists', as described here? In what way do you think having such a simple lifestyle would help Buddhists to gain happiness?**

Buddhist monks and nuns meditate to achieve *nibbana*, the state of peace that comes after greed, illusion and hatred have been overcome. Ajahn Sumedho, a *bhikku* at Amaravati Buddhist Centre in Britain, gives talks on meditation practice. In one of them he had this to say:

'This country is a generous and benevolent country, but we just take it for granted and exploit it for what we can get. We do not think about giving anything to it much. We demand a lot, wanting the government to make everything nice for us, and then we criticise them when they cannot do it. Nowadays you find selfish individuals living their lives on their own terms, without wisely reflecting and living in a way that would be a blessing to the society as a whole. As human beings we can make our lives into great blessings, or we can become a plague on the landscape, taking the Earth's resources for personal gain and getting as much as we can for ourselves, for 'me' and 'mine'.

'In the practice of the *dharma* the sense of 'me' and 'mine' starts to fade away – the sense of 'me' and 'mine' as this little creature here that has a mouth and has to eat. If I just follow the desires of my body and emotions, then I become a greedy, selfish little creature. But when I reflect on the nature of my physical condition and how it can be skilfully used in this lifetime for the welfare of all sentient beings, then this being becomes a blessing.'

From *Mindfulness: The Path to the Deathless*, talks by Ajahn Sumedho

Helping with food preparation at Amaravati

Q **Buddhists have five rules for living by, called the Five Precepts, which comprise: not killing living things, not taking anything that is not given, not speaking falsely, and not indulging in sensual pleasure or taking drink or drugs. How would these rules affect our lifestyle, if everyone in Britain kept to them?**

LIFESTYLES

What improves the quality of life?

We have been looking at what 'the good life' means to different people. For some, it has to do with comfort and material possessions, what we might call 'standard of living'. For others, it has to do with the quality of life, with satisfactions that come from other sources. We have also seen that we have some choices about the way we live. So it follows that we have choices about the ways in which we improve the quality of our lives, too.

Q *What could be done to improve the quality of your life right now?*

There are many different aspects of life that can be improved. For instance, there is personal life, family life, community life, national life and global life. Or you could divide things up another way and talk about improvements in health, housing, education, security, food and drink, transport, working conditions and so on. Politicians are often concerned with such matters.

Behind any idea of improvement there lies a belief, or sometimes more than one belief. Let's take some different examples of beliefs which affect ways in which people choose to improve the quality of life.

> Danny's last wheelchair had far fewer useful gadgets. His friends and family clubbed together to help provide him with a really good one so that he could take part in more games. Many of these friends were Jewish. Jewish people follow the commandment 'Love your fellow as yourself' (Leviticus 19:18). They also try to help people in such a way that they can help themselves in future.

The Hebrew word for charity is *tzedakah*, which also means 'justice'. For Jews this means that giving something to help others who are less fortunate is not just something you do because it is nice and makes you feel good, but because it is righting a wrong.

Q *Can you think of any other improvements to the quality of life that involve helping people to help themselves?*

Q *Can you think of any examples where improving the quality of life for someone, or for a whole community, might be doing justice, or righting a wrong?*

LIFESTYLES

The Leprosy Mission is an international Christian organisation which helps to heal people with leprosy in 35 countries. Leprosy is a disease which affects the nerves. It is not very infectious, but if untreated, loss of feelings in the hands, feet and face can in turn lead to injury to the parts which feel no pain, and so to ugly deformities. In some parts of the world, leprosy sufferers are rejected by their families, who are afraid of the disease.

The Reverend Tony Lloyd, Executive Director for TLM England and Wales, explains:

'As a medical mission our work centres on the cure and rehabilitation of the victims of leprosy. Our surgeons can restore the use of hands, feet and eyes damaged by leprosy. Our nurses and paramedical workers care for patients, our physio- and occupational therapists help them to regain the use of damaged limbs and to relearn vital skills for life in the community.

'However we are not simply a medical mission: we are a Christian medical mission. Where we are able, we not only prolong life but impart life; the eternal life in Christ which is of a Kingdom, beginning in this world, but not of it, and going on beyond this life into eternity. What greater can one do then, when confronted by a deformed patient, rejected by family and friends simply because of an illness, than to offer care of the body and healing of the soul?

Christ has given us the task not only to prolong life but also to impart it.'

Young people in India recovering from leprosy

Q **Leprosy Mission staff obviously want to improve the quality of their patients' health. They also want to improve their patients' lives in another way: what is it?**

Everyone may agree that something needs doing to improve the quality of some aspect of life, but they may disagree on what exactly should be done. Is the improvement we want to make so important that we can choose any course of action to achieve it? Can 'the end always justify the means'?

Adolf Hitler, leader of Germany in the 1930s, wanted to improve the economic and social life of Germans, but the means he chose to achieve this end included what he called the 'final solution': the deliberate murder of all Jews, as well as many others he wrongly blamed for causing Germany's problems. While many agreed with his aim of improving life in Germany, this end clearly did not justify the means.

Q **Does the end ever justify the means? Can you think of any other examples of situations where it did not?**

Q **What if someone were starving, and could only live if they stole food: would the end (staying alive) justify the means (stealing) then?**

LIFESTYLES

What threatens the good life?

In order to provide ourselves with better housing and food, more clothes and possessions, we are using up the world's resources at an ever-increasing rate. For instance, at current rates of tree felling, most of the temperate rainforest in Canada will disappear within the next ten years. The wood goes to the building and paper industries.

Many people think that if we are to enjoy the freedom to live as we wish, we must also be responsible for looking after the world for those who come after us. This means not only other humans, but animals and plants too.

Q **Do you agree? Can you list some specific responsibilities you think we might have?**

'Think globally, act locally' is an environmentalists' slogan. We can recognise the problems on a large scale, but doing something about them could involve every one of us acting locally, here and now. Sometimes it is easier to have a belief than to put it into practice.

Q **In what aspects of our lifestyles do our beliefs clash with what we actually do?**

Tree affected by acid rain pollution

Hundreds of thousands of Kurdish people live as refugees in the mountains of northern Iraq, where they fled from the Iraqi army in 1991. Many have died because they lacked shelter from the heavy winter snows.

Sometimes, things that we do to achieve one goal cause problems in other areas. For instance, we may go to war because we think that the aims of that war justify it. But wars usually leave behind people who are homeless, starving or have no clean water to drink, people who are sick or wounded, and people in prison. And there are many people who, for one reason or another, are in similar trouble in our own country today.

Q **Do we have any responsibility for improving the lifestyles of people in distress, or should we just get on with our own lives? If we do have a responsibility, what kinds of things could we do about it?**

Some religious communities feel strongly that we do have such responsibilities. Practising Muslims, for instance, regularly give $2\frac{1}{2}\%$ of their income (after caring for their own dependents) as *zakat*, an offering to help the local community and the poor and needy.

We know that everybody needs housing, food and water, health and at least some freedom in order to live at all. But simply living, with reasonable health and basic needs taken care of, may not make you happy.

Q **What more do people need to give them a satisfying lifestyle?**

We have seen that people of all the major religions believe that there is more to life than just 'the here and now' and that 'the good life' is not only about having a nice standard of living while we are alive. Many also believe that what we choose to do while we are alive may affect our future lives or our life after death.

Christians, Jews and Muslims believe that the life of our spirit or soul continues after our deaths. Buddhists and Hindus believe that our spirit will return to earth to live further lives in other forms. Either way, it is possible to choose a good path through life or a bad one. Perhaps this is why most religions provide basic rules for believers to live by, to make it more simple to live 'the good life'. We will be looking at rules in the next section.

Q **What choices of lifestyle might threaten a believer's chances of a 'good life' after death (or their progress towards liberation from the cycle of lives and deaths, if they are Hindu)?**

Many people believe that there is an active, evil force that helps to lure people into making the wrong choices in life. In Islam, for example, the Qur'an tells this story:

> When Allah created the first man, he asked all the angels to bow down to the man. The angel Shaitan refused: he thought himself nobler than the man. After all, Allah had created him from fire, and the man from clay. As he would not bow down, Allah cursed Shaitan until the Day of Reckoning; but Shaitan asked for a reprieve, which Allah granted. Then Shaitan swore to spend his days luring all, except Allah's most faithful servants, into evil. Allah then promised Shaitan that Hell would be filled with his offspring and those who followed him.
>
> Adapted from The Qur'an, *Sad* 38: 67-88

Satan, or the Devil, as he is traditionally imagined in the West

Q **Is evil the result of what people choose to do, or can evil be caused by evil forces of any kind? Find out what different religions have to say about this.**

6 RULES

Why do we have rules?

There are times when we all feel like breaking a few rules. But imagine a world in which there are no rules or laws at all. Everyone has complete freedom to do as they wish all the time. You can cycle on the right or the left-hand side of the road, whichever you feel like. Say you want something you have seen in a shop. Or you desperately want to win a game. Or you hate somebody. What would there be to stop you stealing and cheating, injuring or even killing?

Q *Would a world without rules or laws be possible? Would you like to live in such a place?*

Q *Make a list of any sets of rules that you follow. Which ones do you have to follow, and which do you choose to follow? Do any sets of rules contain some you would like to change?*

So why do we have rules and laws? That depends on which rules and laws we are talking about. In this section, we will look at some rules, and what beliefs lie behind them. We will ask how rules are used, and whether there are some rules that never change. And we will see what happens when rules are broken, and what happens to rule-breakers.

Take the game of tennis. There is no point in playing a game of tennis unless you stick to the rules: in a sense, the game *is* the rules. Some rules limit a particular activity in such a way that we are free to do it safely and effectively; for instance, the rules of the road for traffic. Many of our civil and criminal rules – our laws – ensure that our freedom to do things does not limit other people's freedom to do what they want to.

Some rules help to define a particular group: if you want to be a part of the group, you keep the rules. For instance, if you are a Scout or Guide, you wear a uniform and make certain promises. Sikhs, too, wear a kind of uniform of head covering, comb, steel bracelet, sword and special underclothes. Each item helps to remind the wearer of a particular aspect of being a Sikh. Each has a name beginning with K, so they are known as the Five Ks.

Q *Think of a club or group that you belong to. What are the rules for belonging to that group? What purpose do the rules serve?*

Many people believe that there are, or should be, a few broad general rules about the way we live, which should be true for all people, no matter what their beliefs. We could call these rules 'moral' or 'ethical' rules. They are about how we relate to each other and to the world about us. There have been many attempts to define such general rules. One recent example is the United Nations Declaration of Human Rights. Earlier ones include those of the major religions.

The authority for such moral rules is thought to lie beyond human agreements about what is useful or practical. For instance, it is said that murder is wrong not only because humans agree that it would be more convenient if people could not get away with killing each other, but because murder is always and absolutely wrong. When asked why they believe this, many people will say it is God's law.

However, people may still argue about many aspects of rules: about the authority behind them, about exactly what they mean, and about how they are to be applied.

THE NOAHIDE CODE

Jews believe that the following rules for standards of behaviour, set for Noah and his family in his agreement with God, should be rules for all human beings to follow, regardless of their faith – though Jews should also keep further commandments.

1 To have one God
2 Not to show contempt or disrespect for God
3 Not to have sex with anyone you are not married to
4 Not to steal
5 Not to murder
6 To practise justice
7 To be kind to animals

Q *Which, if any, of these rules do you consider the most important? Are there any that you find surprising? Would you add anything to the list?*

Many religious people find that living their lives according to a set of rules is not restrictive but actually brings them greater freedom. Muslims, for example, practise five duties which are often called 'the Five Pillars of Islam'. They include declaring their faith in Allah, praying five times every day, fasting in the month of Ramadan, giving to people in need, and, if they can, at least once in their lives making the pilgrimage to Makkah. The outward keeping of these rules reflects their inner beliefs, and helps develop qualities of character that Muslims believe are pleasing to Allah. Through obedience, they achieve peace.

Q *What kinds of beliefs about life are to be found in the Muslim rules? How would keeping to the rules help to develop a good character? Do rules help us to become better people?*

RULES

What do the rules really mean?

It is quite possible to have one rule and lots of opinions about how it should be put into practice. Our system of law shows this very well. In their training, lawyers have to learn about all the ways in which judges have interpreted particular laws in the past, because these examples are the best way of finding out what the law means for their client's case.

Q *Can you think of any examples from your own experience of rules which can be applied in more than one way?*

For Muslims it is a basic rule that the human body should be decently covered. Some details of dress are prescribed by the Qur'an and *hadith* (traditional sayings), but people interpret them differently.

SAMIRA

'The Qur'an says women must cover themselves from neck to ankle, and cover their heads and hair, and that we should wear an outer covering to go out. I think following the rules is an important part of being a Muslim. It is not our business to question them.'

NADIA

'I think the Qur'an asks us to dress modestly. I do that, but I also like to fit in with my friends. I think that the passages about dress in the Qur'an show the Prophet's concern about women. The main thing is that we should not dress only to attract men, because that could lead to harm.'

Both girls here are following the same rules in their own way. Both will point to passages from the Qur'an to back up their point of view. Samira feels that the rules are to be obeyed without question because they are Allah's, while Nadia feels that the purpose behind the rules must be more important than the details.

Q *Are there any rules which you obey without questioning the authority behind them? How do you decide which rules absolutely must be obeyed, and which can be questioned?*

Sometimes, when people are trying to decide how a rule applies to their particular circumstances, they will make a distinction between the 'letter of the law' and the 'spirit of the law'. That is, they will try to look behind the rule to find the general principle or belief on which it is based.

In the Christian Bible story, Jesus is shown as having done this in his activities on the Sabbath day. Jewish law holds that no work is to be done on the Sabbath because this 'seventh day' was the day on which God commanded people to rest, in memory of his creation of the world in six days. Some people, who objected to Jesus's teachings, wanted to catch him breaking this law.

> 'On another occasion when he went to the synagogue, there was a man in the congregation who had a withered arm; and they were watching to see whether Jesus would cure him on the Sabbath, so that they could bring a charge against him. He said to the man with the withered arm, 'Come and stand out here'. Then he turned to them: 'Is it permitted to do good or to do evil on the Sabbath, to save life or to kill?' They had nothing to say; and, looking round at them with anger and sorrow at their obstinate stupidity, he said to the man 'Stretch out your arm.'
>
> He stretched it out and his arm was restored.'
>
> Mark 3:1-5

Q **In this example, what was the 'letter of the law' and what did Jesus seem to think was the 'spirit of the law'?**

Q **Can you give any examples from your own experience of having to distinguish between the letter and the spirit of the law?**

Jesus, who was born a Jew and was familiar with the Ten Commandments and with other laws of the Jewish tradition, said these two commandments from the Torah were the most important of them all.

> 'The first is: "Hear O Israel: the Lord our God is the only Lord; Love the Lord your God with all your heart, with all your soul, with all your mind and with all your strength." The second is this: "Love your neighbour as you love yourself." There is no other commandment greater than these.'
>
> Mark 12: 30-31

Q **What does this rule actually mean in practice for Christians? Can you find some examples of how it is interpreted in modern life?**

RULES

Are there any rules which never change?

Rules and laws in general reflect the circumstances of the time at which they were made. For instance, the Bible commandment that 'You shall not covet [envy] your neighbour's house; you shall not covet your neighbour's wife, his slave, his slave-girl, his ox, his ass or anything that belongs to him' (Exodus 20:17) was obviously written at a time when most householders were men, and men who had slaves and oxen, among other things! Often, though, it is possible to see what the rule would be if it were to be written today.

Q *How would you interpret the commandment above in today's world? Choose some modern examples of things (or people) that might be objects of envy. Do we, today, think of envy as something bad, as a sin?*

Rules are often changed and updated. You can probably think of some rules that have been changed in your lifetime. For instance, what was the rule about your bedtime when you were five, and what is it now? Rules are changed to fit changing circumstances.

It is the same with laws. Once, there were all sorts of laws governing the use of horse-drawn vehicles on the roads. Now these have been replaced by rules about vehicles with internal combustion engines instead, and new ones have been invented to take account of the invention of motorways. Circumstances change, and the need for new rules arises.

Sometimes rules are changed because people begin to see things differently. For instance at one time in Britain only men could vote. Gradually, a few women persuaded others to see that this was unjust, and that women should be represented in parliament too. It took a lot of protest to get the law changed, as it was in 1928. These days nearly everyone over 18 can vote.

People campaigning for the 'one person, one vote' rule to be applied in South Africa.

Q *Do you know of any other laws that have changed? What is the belief behind the idea that everyone should have one vote? Are there any unjust rules that you would like to see changed?*

RULES

Many people believe that some rules are absolute and never change, no matter what changes in society take place over time. Some of these rules are expressed in the central commandments of the great faiths. We have already looked at the Noahide Code of Judaism and, in the last section, at the Five Precepts of Buddhism. The Ten Commandments, which the Bible story says were given by God to the prophet Moses, are generally accepted by many Jews and Christians. They are to be found in Exodus 20.

Some of these absolute rules are ones that a great many people, believers and non-believers, agree on. But what does such a rule mean in practice? Let's look at one example.

THE SIXTH COMMANDMENT: 'YOU SHALL NOT COMMIT MURDER.'

'I could never kill another human being in any circumstances. I believe life is sacred: God gives it and God takes it away. For that reason, I can't agree with abortion, for example – women do not have the right to choose to take an unborn child's life.'

'Murder means taking the life of another person. I don't think of an embryo as a person – the mother's life is always more important at that stage.'

'I think that in war time, killing is justified. You have to be fighting in defence of important values, though – not for selfish aims like gaining more land.'

'If I had a close relative in a coma on a life support machine, and there was no hope of their getting better, I would agree to turn off the switch.'

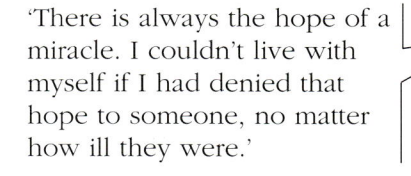

'There is always the hope of a miracle. I couldn't live with myself if I had denied that hope to someone, no matter how ill they were.'

'I'm a pacifist. I don't believe there is any cause which justifies the taking of human life. I am prepared to die myself rather than kill anyone else.'

'What about animals? Isn't it murder to kill them, too?'

'I don't think animal lives are as important as human lives.'

Q **Read the rest of the Ten Commandments in the Bible (Exodus 20). Which ones do many people break? Which ones do people apply differently? Are there some that seem to be more important than others?**

RULES

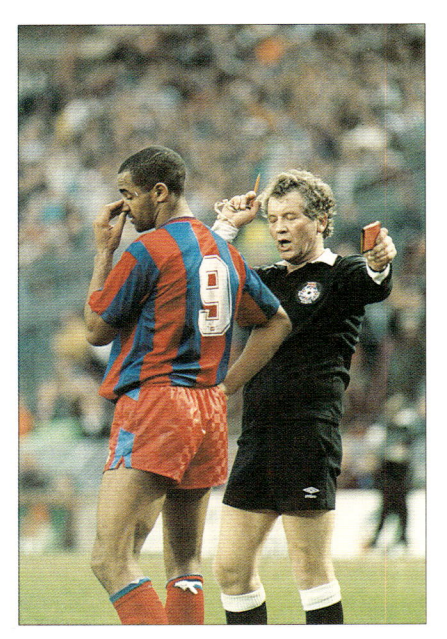

The referee decides a player has broken the rules

What happens to rule breakers?

What do we do with people who freely choose to break rules? It is a fairly simple matter in the case of a game. Since the game is the rules, if you are not keeping the rules you are not playing the game. Either a penalty is awarded against you, or you are excluded from the game: 'sent off'.

Q *We are often angry with people who break rules. Why should this be?*

Often, we punish people who break rules. You may have had your pocket money stopped for doing something wrong: as an adult, you can be fined for breaking certain laws. Fines are usually imposed for offences that are considered less serious, such as parking in the wrong place. You may have been sent to your room for doing something adults consider 'a serious offence'. Under our laws, offenders such as persistent robbers or murderers may be punished with a prison sentence. In prison, people are separated from their families and friends and live in cramped spaces in unpleasant conditions.

Q *What is the aim of punishing someone who breaks the law? Is it to make them pay for their wrong-doing by suffering? To stop them doing the same thing again in future?*

At one time, British law allowed death by hanging as a punishment for murder. The maximum penalty is now life imprisonment. There have also been calls for the reform of the prison system. Reformers want to see a move away from a system of punishment and towards a system of 'rehabilitation'. Prisoners would use their time in prison to acquire social skills and training for work, in the hope that they will then be less likely to commit crimes again.

Q *Do you think that punishment should be emphasized for law-breakers, or rehabilitation?*

Forgiveness is also part of the system of justice. First-time offenders may be dismissed with a warning not to do it again. Juries will sometimes find people 'not guilty' because, although they did actually commit the crime of which they are accused, the jury members think they have already suffered enough – women who have killed men who have beaten and abused them for years, for example. Youngsters may be put 'on probation', with a social worker to look after them, rather than being sent to prison or Borstal.

Q *What sorts of things make us want to forgive rule breakers?*

The idea of punishment after our deaths for sin or wrong-doing in our lifetimes is to be found in some of the major world religions. Often, the place of punishment, or hell, is seen as the opposite of the reward in heaven waiting for the faithful believer who has kept to the rules.

Some believers say that these descriptions are only a way of putting into words an experience that it is not really possible to describe. For them, separation from God's loving presence is a kind of hell, and being one with him is heaven.

Hindus also see life in this way. The aim of human life is to achieve *moksha* or liberation from the cycles of birth and death. If we persist in wrong actions, we stay trapped in those cycles and never know the bliss of unity with Brahman, or God. The Hindu snakes and ladders game shows the kinds of action that will help people to progress.

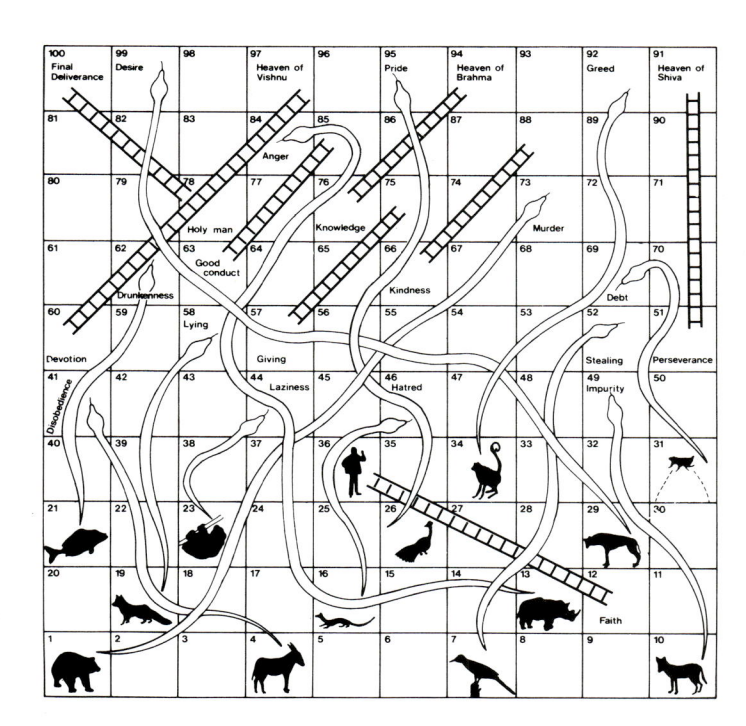

Q **Do you know about the ideas Christians and Muslims have about the afterlife? Don't forget that not all people of the same faith believe exactly the same things. In each religion, how are people to be judged?**

Forgiveness is seen as God's mercy in many religions. In Islam, for example, all actions are carefully classified by the Shari'ah, or Islamic laws, so that Muslims may, in theory, know exactly what to do in all circumstances, and also know the consequences if they do not do what is right. However, even those who disobey the laws are offered a path back to God if they 'repent'. Repentance, for a Muslim, means:

1 Knowing that one has done wrong
2 Feeling sorry that one has done wrong
3 Deciding never to do it again
4 Praying for God's forgiveness and help in resisting evil.

> Forgiveness is a also central part of Christian belief. Jesus taught his followers to pray saying:
> 'Father, thy name be hallowed
> Thy kingdom come
> Give us each day our daily bread
> *And forgive us our sins*
> *For we too forgive all who have done us wrong*
> And do not bring us to the test.'
>
> Luke 11: 1-4

7 SUFFERING

What is suffering?

Pain, in its many forms, is all about us. There is physical pain, and there is mental pain. We suffer from not getting what we want, and from having things we don't want. In this section, we shall be looking at different kinds of suffering, and asking questions about what suffering is, why it happens, and whether it has any purpose.

> At the end of the island I noticed a small green frog. He was exactly half in and half out of the water, looking like a schematic diagram of an amphibian, and he didn't jump. He didn't jump; I crept closer. At last I knelt on the island's winterkilled grass, lost, dumbstruck, staring at the frog in the creek just four feet away. He was a very small frog with wide, dull eyes. And just as I looked at him, he slowly crumpled and began to sag. The spirit vanished from his eyes as if snuffed. His skin emptied and drooped; his very skull seemed to collapse and settle like a kicked tent. He was shrinking before my eyes like a deflating football. I watched the taut, glistening skin on his shoulders ruck, and rumple, and fall. Soon, part of his skin, formless as a pricked balloon, lay in floating folds like a bright scum on top of the water: it was a monstrous and terrifying thing. I gaped bewildered, appalled. An oval shadow hung in the water behind the drained frog; then the shadow glided away. The frog bag started to sink.
>
> I had read about the giant water bug, but never seen one. 'Giant water bug' is really the name of the creature, which is an enormous, heavy bodied brown beetle. It eats insects, tadpoles, fishes and frogs. Its grasping forelegs are mighty and hooked inward. It seizes a victim with these legs, hugs it tight and paralyzes it with enzymes injected during a vicious bite. That one bite is the only bite it ever takes. Through the puncture shoot the poisons that dissolve the victim's muscles and bones and organs – all but the skin – and through it the giant water bug sucks out the victim's body, reduced to a juice.
>
> From *Pilgrim at Tinker Creek* by Annie Dillard

The world is full of eating and being eaten, much of which involves suffering and pain. Benefit to one creature often involves pain or death for another.

Q *Do you think of nature as kind and beautiful, or cruel and ugly, or a mixture of the two? Can you think of some examples to support both points of view?*

Human beings experience pain and suffering throughout life. We are subject to illness and injury, and we must inevitably die. Although we spend a lot of our time trying to improve the quality of our lives, as we have seen, we still have to come to terms with the fact that suffering exists.

SUFFERING

This Irish plane crashed on the edge of the M1 motorway

We spend quite a lot of our time fascinated by suffering in its many forms. When a big accident happens, such as a plane crash or an earthquake or a flood, people want to stop and look. We watch the news on television and wince as we hear the daily details of injuries, suffering and death. But we leave the set on. Newspapers, magazines and TV soap operas thrive on stories of disasters, crimes and broken relationships.

Q *Why are we so interested in painful events that happen to others?*

When something painful happens closer to home, and we are involved, we also suffer. Perhaps a member of our family develops a life-threatening disease such as leukaemia. Or maybe a much-loved grandparent has a disabling stroke and becomes paralysed, confined to a wheelchair. A marriage or friendship breaking up can sometimes be just as painful as a physical injury, too. When such events take place, we have to find ways to respond to them. They call on our deepest resources and make us examine our beliefs about the nature of life.

As if diseases and accidents and old age and death were not enough to cope with, people have invented many more ways of causing suffering. What about persecution, torture and imprisonment? Poverty? The abuse of children? Wars, and the destruction and famine they involve?

In this section we shall be looking at different aspects of suffering, raising questions about them, and noting some of the responses to it found in the world's religions.

Q *Make a list of all the different kinds of suffering you can think of. Now underline any that are caused only by human beings. Are the others outside our control?*

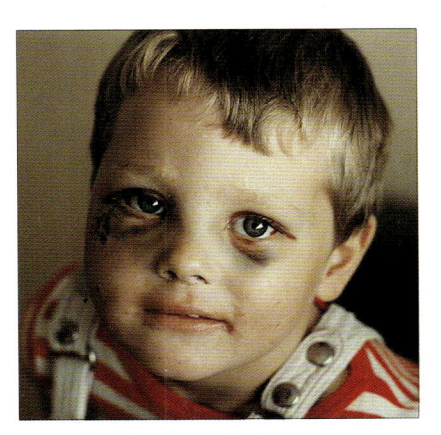

What makes people hurt young children?

SUFFERING

Has suffering a place?

There seems to be a lot of suffering in life. What part does it play? When we start to examine suffering more closely, some of it at least seems to be a part of the natural order. The giant water bug we read about on p.56 has to eat frogs in order to survive; the frog itself had been busily eating worms and flies. Equally, we eat plants and animals which have grown by fuelling themselves with other creatures. When we die, our bodies return to earth and nourish bacteria and plants which serve as food for other beings.

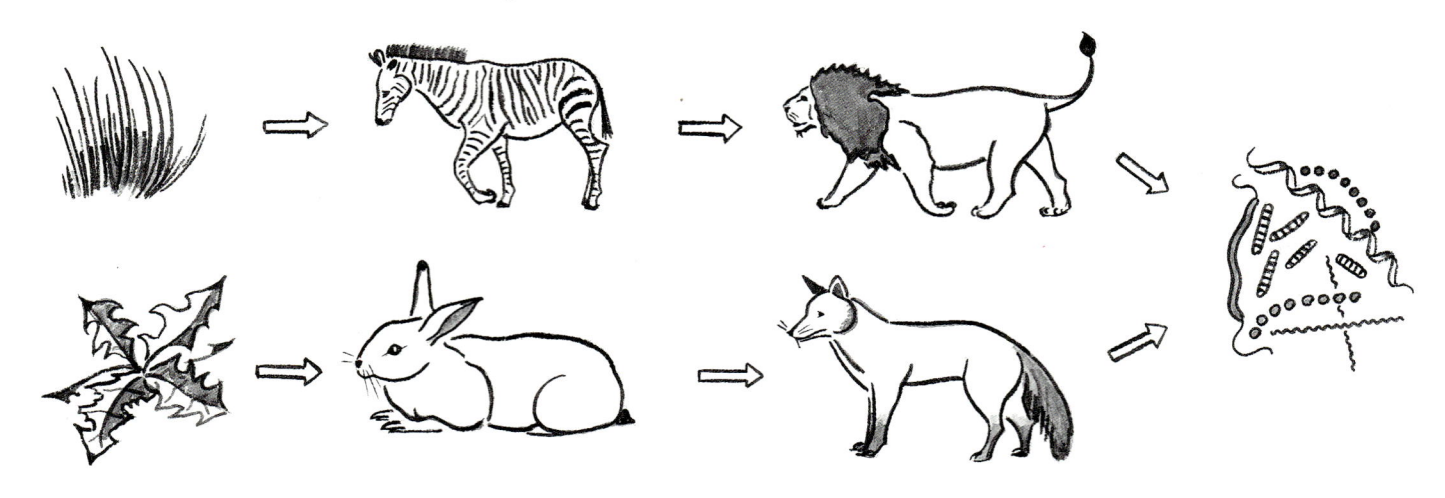

Q *Does the fact that we are taking part in a greater, natural process make you feel differently about the suffering of individual humans or animals?*

Pain can also have a useful role in alerting us to injury and disease. An ache in your lower back may mean that you are lifting weights that are too heavy for you, or lifting them in the wrong way. A series of headaches may mean that your eyes are straining and that you need glasses. In the same way, mental suffering can be a signal that we need to do something about the way we are living, or thinking. It can be the spur that makes us move towards something better.

Q *What kinds of experiences have helped you to grow up or to understand life? Have any of them involved suffering?*

Many women describe labour and childbirth as the worst pain they have ever suffered, but say it was worth it to have the baby at the end. Pain seems to be bound up with the creation of the new. People who create in another way, such as artists, musicians and actors, sometimes talk of the pain and suffering involved in the effort of creating their paintings, concerts or performances. We talk about 'taking pains' to do something properly.

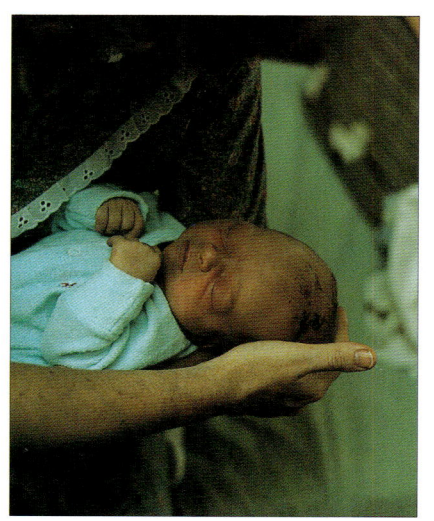

All of us came into the world through the pain of childbirth

SUFFERING

The idea of birth, or rebirth, is often used as a way of talking about spiritual progress, too. Christians sometimes talk of being 'reborn' after an encounter with Jesus Christ. Many will contrast the newfound joy of their 'rebirth' with the pain and suffering of the period before. Some will see the pain as a necessary struggle which always preceeds growth and the coming of the new.

Q **Is suffering a necessary part of our growth? Could we do without it altogether?**

Buddhists certainly believe that suffering has a place in the world. For them, suffering is an inevitable part of being alive. They call it *dukkha*, a word which expresses 'dis-ease' and restlessness as much as suffering. The Buddha's teaching is expressed in statements known as the Four Noble Truths:

1 Life is unsatisfactory
2 *Dukkha* arises
3 *Dukkha* can cease
4 The way is laid down in the Noble Eightfold Path

For Buddhists, suffering means always wanting something else. If you are ill, you want to be well; if you are poor, you want to be rich; if you are hot, you want to be cool. They believe we are living under the illusion that it is possible to reach a state in which we have everything we want, and rid ourselves of everything we don't want. The 'Eightfold Path' suggests ways of behaving which will lead beyond this illusion, and give us peace and calm, and eventually 'enlightenment'.

> When the Buddha was alive, a woman called Kisogotama came to see him on the advice of a follower of his. Kisogotama's only child had just died and she was full of grief. She had been carrying the little dead body from one house to another, searching for someone who could heal her beloved child.
>
> The Buddha told her that if he was to restore the child, she would have to bring him four or five poppy seeds. But, he told her, the seeds must be given her by people whose homes death had never entered.
>
> Kisogotama set out on her desperate search. Again she went to one home after another, but not one could she find that had never been visited by death. After a while she realised what Buddha had taught her. She buried her child and returned to him to become one of his followers.
>
> Traditional Buddhist story

Q **What do you think Kisogotama learned on her search for the poppy seeds? Do you think that it is possible to live without suffering?**

SUFFERING

Can suffering be a means to an end?

Everyone knows that some goals are only achieved through effort. If we want to get fit, we must work hard at our exercises. At first, it will hurt; but we know we must break through the pain barrier and carry on until we see some results. If we want to take up a particular career, we must pass exams; and that means hard work, too.

Part of this effort may also involve giving up things we might otherwise enjoy. For instance, athletes preparing for important races have to spend all their waking hours in training. They are only allowed to eat the kinds of food that are good for muscles and stamina. There is little time for friends and family, or pastimes like the movies or discos. They have to be in bed by 9.00 p.m. every night, including weekends. Why do they do this? Because the goal of winning the race is more important to them than anything else.

If you want to climb Mount Everest, you will not only need to be fit physically. You will also have to be prepared to suffer extreme cold, possibly frostbite, and to risk death by falling off cliffs and into crevasses.

Q *What sorts of goals make people willing to suffer in order to attain them? Can you think of other examples from the worlds of science, or the arts, or exploration?*

Some people are also prepared to make this sort of effort for religious reasons. This kind of suffering can have a very wide range in practice. For instance, Christians may decide to give up something they normally enjoy – cakes, or sweets perhaps – for the six weeks before Easter, called Lent. They do this in order to help them think more deeply about their faith and deepen their commitment to it. Lent is a time of repentance for past shortcomings, in preparation for the renewal of Easter.

Jim decided to give blood a few years ago when he heard that hospitals were in need of more donors.

'I've never had an operation myself or anything (touch wood!) I've always been very healthy. I put it down to all those chip butties I ate as a kid! No, I just felt that this was something I could do to help, so I just went down and did it. It doesn't hurt, and they give you a nice cup of tea and a biscuit afterwards.'

SUFFERING

The satisfaction that Jim gets from being a blood donor comes from the feeling that he is giving something to other people. Although his blood is precious to him, he is willing to sacrifice that and endure the discomfort of having it taken, because he thinks that there is a greater need than his own. This kind of self-sacrifice can appear in many different forms. It can involve giving up money, possessions and time as well as blood. There are many causes that people choose to give to, and many ideals that they sacrifice themselves for.

Q *Do you know of any other examples of people who have given up something of their own for a greater good?*

Some believers may even deliberately inflict some physical discomfort on themselves. This can be done as a form of punishment to themselves, as a way of saying sorry to God for their sins. For Catholic Christians, like the lady in our picture, who make pilgrimages to special shrines and places of worship, it is also a way to understand some of the suffering that they believe Jesus undertook at his crucifixion.

A pilgrim at the shrine of Our Lady of Fatima, in Portugal

For Christians, the suffering and death of Jesus on the cross (an instrument of torture) is central to their faith. They believe Jesus was God's only son, and that his death and resurrection was the way God revealed his love for the whole of humanity. For them, this was the supreme example of self-sacrifice. You can read the story of Jesus's arrest, trial and death in the Bible New Testament Gospels, for example in John 18–20.

Q *Do you know what Christians believe about Jesus's suffering, death and resurrection? What purpose do they believe it serves?*

Q *Make a list of all the positive ways in which effort (which might involve pain and suffering) can be used to achieve goals. Which are individual goals, and which are goals for a group ('collective') goals?*

SUFFERING

How can we cope with suffering?

Pain and suffering seem to be facts of life which will not go away. How do we come to terms with them?

As a society, we act together in various ways to reduce pain and suffering. The medical field is one very obvious example. In Britain, medical treatment is generally available for anyone who needs it. We also support research into major illnesses such as cancer and into the genetic conditions which produce illnesses such as cystic fibrosis. And we try to prevent the development of illness through health education, dental checks and eye tests.

Pain and suffering are often located in the body, but they also affect our minds. As we have seen, the quality of our lives can produce suffering, too. Things like good schools, housing and jobs may be just as important to our well-being as medicine.

Q *Can you think of any organisations which promote health and well-being in society?*

Q *What major areas does health education cover?*

Being human, we are often concerned about the suffering of other humans, whether they are members of our own society or of others. Government uses our taxes to provide a certain amount of aid to developing countries. Many people also contribute to charities such as Oxfam, Save the Children or War on Want which help to relieve poverty, create work and improve conditions for those who are suffering.

Q *Name any other charities you know of which help people all over the world. How do they make us aware of suffering? What kinds of suffering do they deal with? What beliefs do they share? Are any based on religious principles?*

People also have to help themselves when they are suffering. To gain the necessary determination to face up to their pain, and to do something about it, or simply to suffer it, can take great courage. Sometimes people need the help and support of others. Sometimes they need to be alone, and to find an inner strength through meditation, or prayer. This may involve struggle and heart-searching. If they are believers, they may ask God to help them come to terms with their problem, or show them a way to deal with it. Others, like the Buddhists, may look into the nature of suffering itself as a way of coming to terms with it.

SUFFERING

A Christian nun once went to become a missionary in Peru. Shortly after she arrived, she fell ill with rheumatoid arthritis, a painful and crippling disease. She went home for an operation on her hands, but then decided to return to Peru.

'I remember thinking that even though my hands were going to be broken and crooked, they would still be sacred to me. I'd use them to bring something to somebody, I didn't know what. My hands could be the compassionate hands of Christ as much as the hands of the doctors and nurses.

'So I sought to be able to enter into the world of the sick, and to live with the mystery of suffering. I saw that I had to enter into my own experience of pain, and to face up to it, and to allow myself to be changed by it. Without that, nothing could be done. I saw that healing comes with owning our wounds as the first step in moving beyond them.

'I returned to Peru at a lower altitude. Almost everything had changed, especially my attitude towards the people I was working with. I could feel their terrible poverty and pain in a whole new way. In fact it seemed as if I was seeing it for the first time. How often I'd rushed around trying to solve people's problems without really seeing them – the pain in their faces, the insecure eyes, the nervous hands, all expressions of the hurt inside. It was only when suffering had actually touched me that I began to feel their condition.'

From *How Can I Help?* by Ram Dass and Paul Gorman

Q **Do you know of any other examples of great courage in the face of suffering? Did this courage come from any particular belief, or help to create such a belief?**

Not everyone experiences suffering as we might imagine. Benares, on the river Ganges in India, is a centre of pilgrimage for many Hindus as well as Buddhists, Jains and Sikhs. Many go there to die because they believe that to have their ashes thrown into the river will release them from rebirth. For this reason, the city seems full of sick and dying people, many of whom are begging. To visitors unaware of the people's beliefs, the suffering can appear terrible. One such visitor learned why the city was sacred to Hindus, and what their beliefs were. He said:

'Now as I placed coins in begging bowls I was able to look into the eyes of the people. And to my profound amazement I found in their eyes not the suffering that I had been reticent to face but looks of peace. In fact I even saw in some of their eyes pity for me, lost as I was in illusion. Leprosy, leukaemia, blindness, such poverty that they had only a loincloth and begging bowl ... and still...peace. How wrong I'd been to assume that they were suffering as I would have been suffering in a similar situation.'

From *How Can I Help?* by Ram Dass and Paul Gorman

People in Benares (also called Varanasi), by the river Ganges

Q **Do you know of any examples of people who accept suffering as part of their lives? How do people decide when to relieve suffering, and when to accept it?**

INDEX

afterlife 33, 39, 55
ahimsa 31
animal rights 13
astrology 12, 38
authority 50

birthdays 16, 20
Baisakhi 17
Benares, see Varanasi
Buddhist community 43

Carnival 18
celebrations 16–23
chance 12–13
charity 62
Christian Aid 30
Christmas 20, 21
conflict 28–29
corn circles 10
creation 9
crucifixion 61

death 35, 47
destiny 12
determinism 13
Devil 13, 47
Diwali 7
dharma 38, 43
dress, and Hasidic Jews 25; and Muslim women 50; and Sikhs 48
dukkha 59

Earth 8
Eid al-Nabi 17
Eid ul-Fitr 19
ends and means 45
envy 52
eternal life 38, 42
ethics 38, 49
evil 47
Exodus 52, 53

faith 13
Five Ks (Sikh dress code) 48
Five Pillars of Islam 49
Five Precepts of Buddhism 43
forces 12
free will 12, 13

freedom 46
forgiveness 54, 55

Gandhi, M K 31
good and evil 47
good life, the 40, 47
Guy Fawkes Day 16
Golden wedding 22

hajj 31, 39
happiness 43, 47
healing 11
heaven 33, 55
hell 33, 55
Hiroshima Day 20
horoscope 12
Holi 23

ihram 31
illusion 10

Jesus and material possessions 42; and healing 11; suffering and crucifixion 61
judgement 35, 42

karma 15, 36
karma yoga 38
Kisogotama 59
Kogi of Colombia 29

laws, see rules
Lent 60
Leprosy Mission, The 45
lifestyles 42, 43, 46

magic 10
Mass 23, 39
meditation 62
miracles 10, 11
moksha 55
morality 28, 38, 49
Mother's Day 22
murder 49

natural world 8–15
nature 56, 58
nibbana 43
Noahide Code 49
non-violence 31
Northern Ireland 28–29

obedience 49

pain, see suffering
patterns in nature 15
Passover 19
pilgrimage to Benares/Varanasi 63; to Makkah 31, 34, 39
possessions 40, 41
predestination 12
protest 52
punishment 39, 54

quality of life 44

racism 30
Rakhi 38
rehabilitation 54
relationships 24–31
responsibility 46–47
right 38
Ramadan 19
Remembrance Day 17
rules 47, 48–55

science 8, 15
Sabbath 51
seder meal 19
self-sacrifice 61
Seven Wonders of the World 14
shahadah 39
Shaitan (Satan) 47
sixth commandment, the 53
spirit or soul 47
suffering 56–63

Ten Commandments, The 51, 53
tzedakah 44

universe 8, 15

Varanasi 63
vocation 39

war 46
wrong 38
wonders of nature 14

zakat 31, 47